HOW TO DRAW
40 ANIMALS IN 12 STEPS

ULTIMATE GUIDE FOR EVERYONE - UNICORNS, TIGERS, LIONS, AND MORE!

CREATED BY
CORINNE LARSEN

HOW TO DRAW 40 ANIMALS IN 12 STEPS
CREATED BY
CORINNE LARSEN
LARSEN FALLS PUBLISHING
@2023 COPYRIGHT

Unicorn

①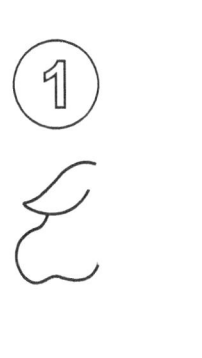

②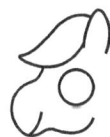

③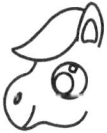

④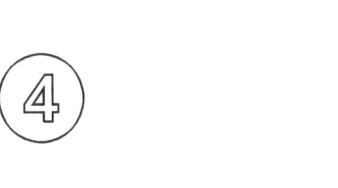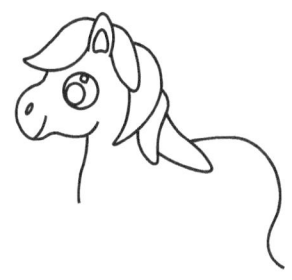

⑤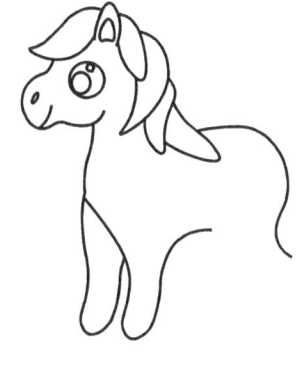

⑥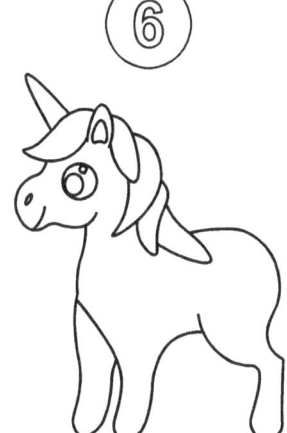

⑦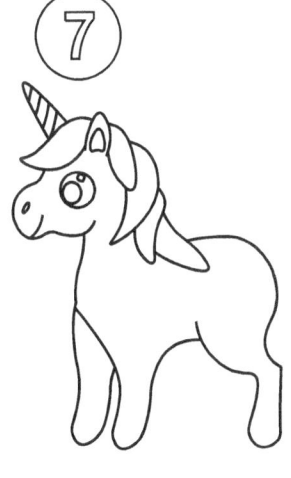

⑧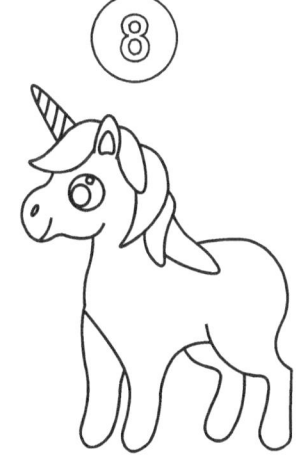

⑨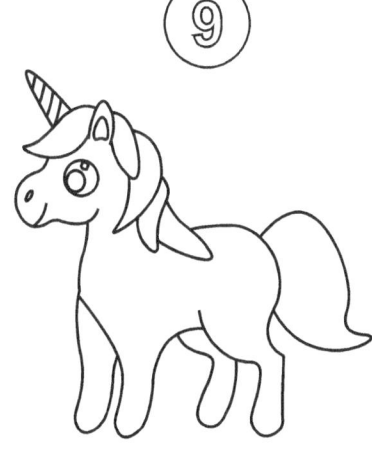

⑩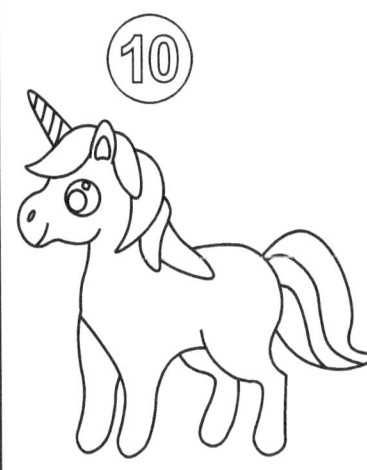

⑪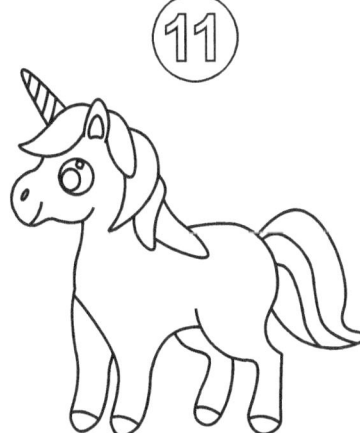

⑫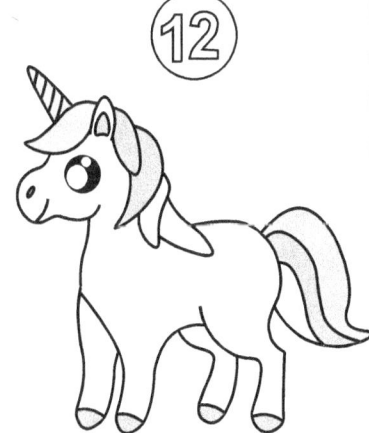

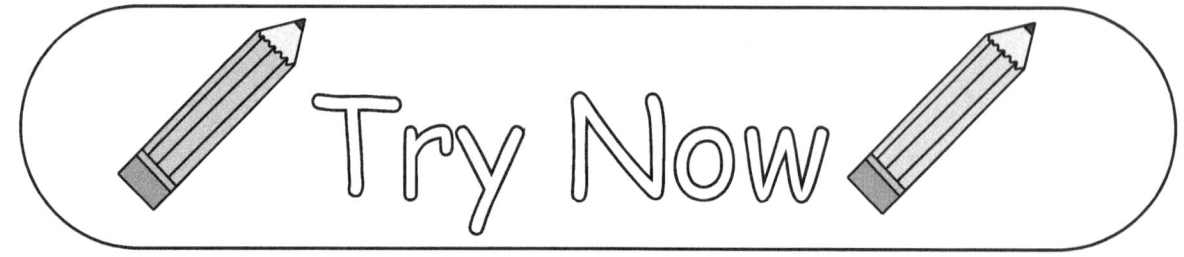

Tiger

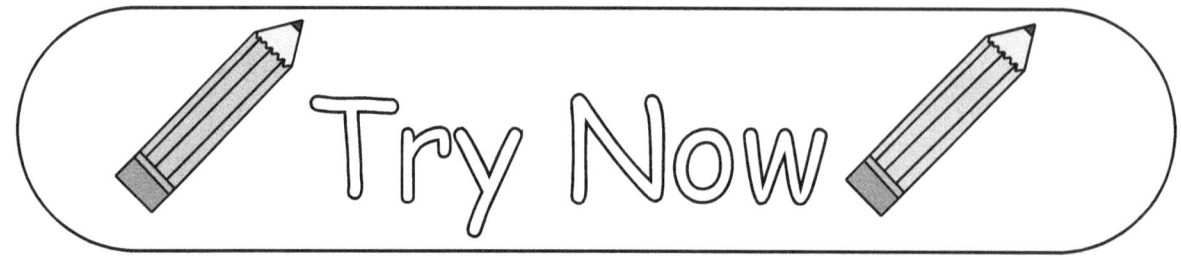

Lion

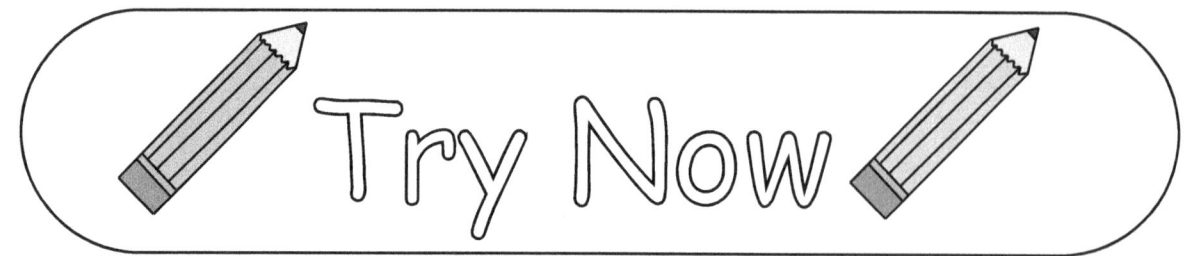

Try Now

Elephant

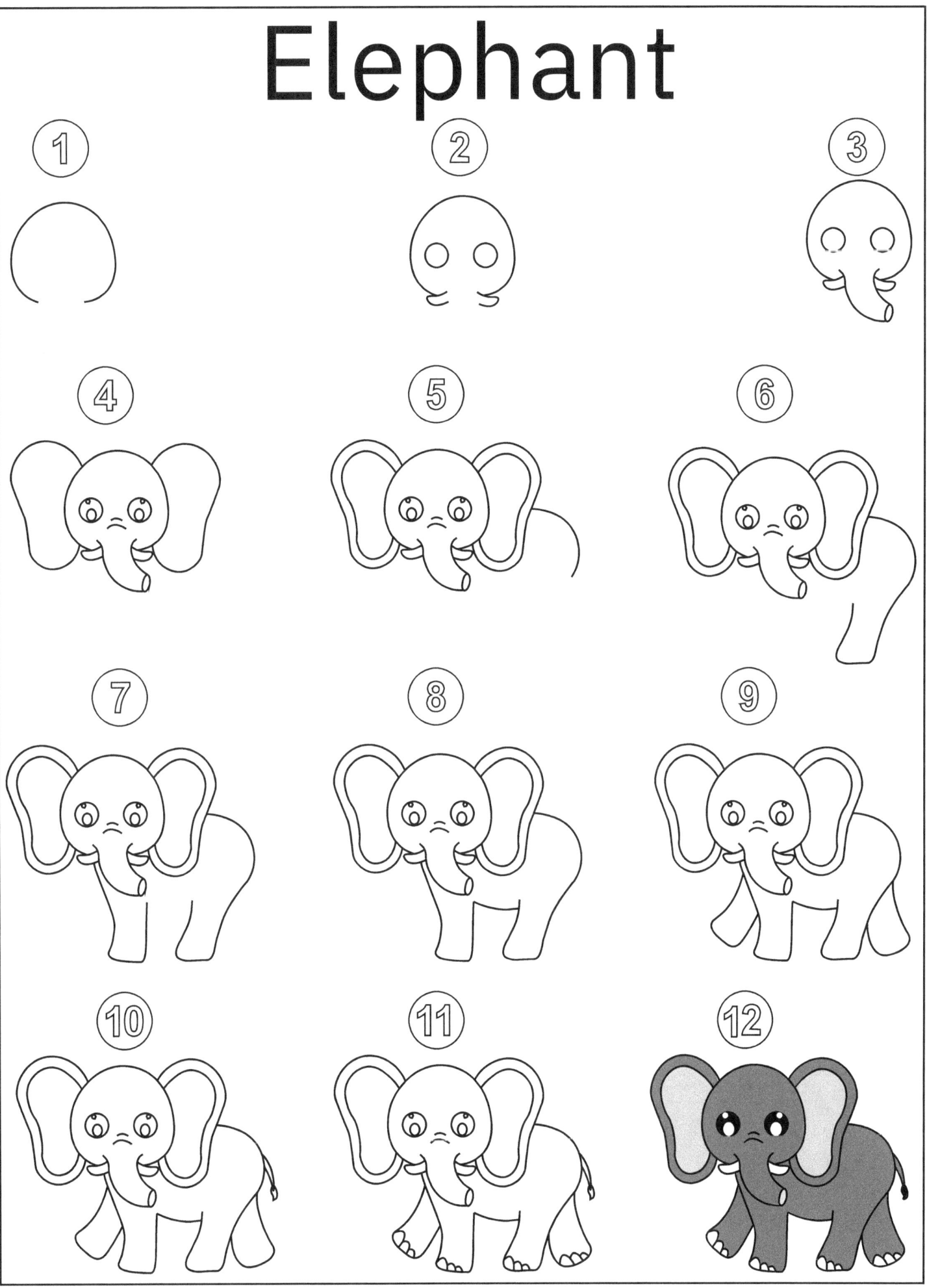

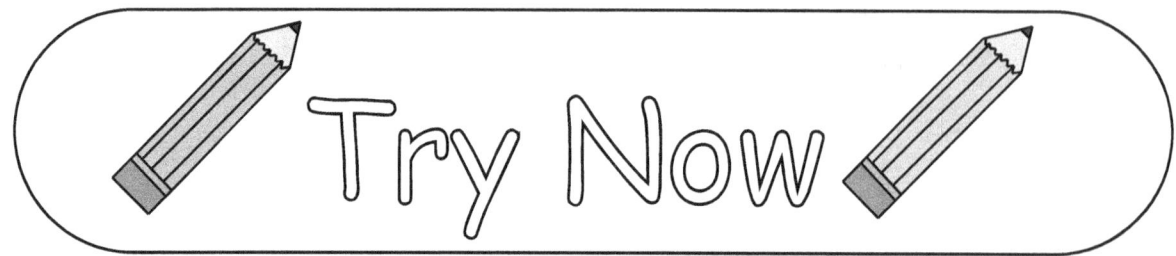

Giraffe

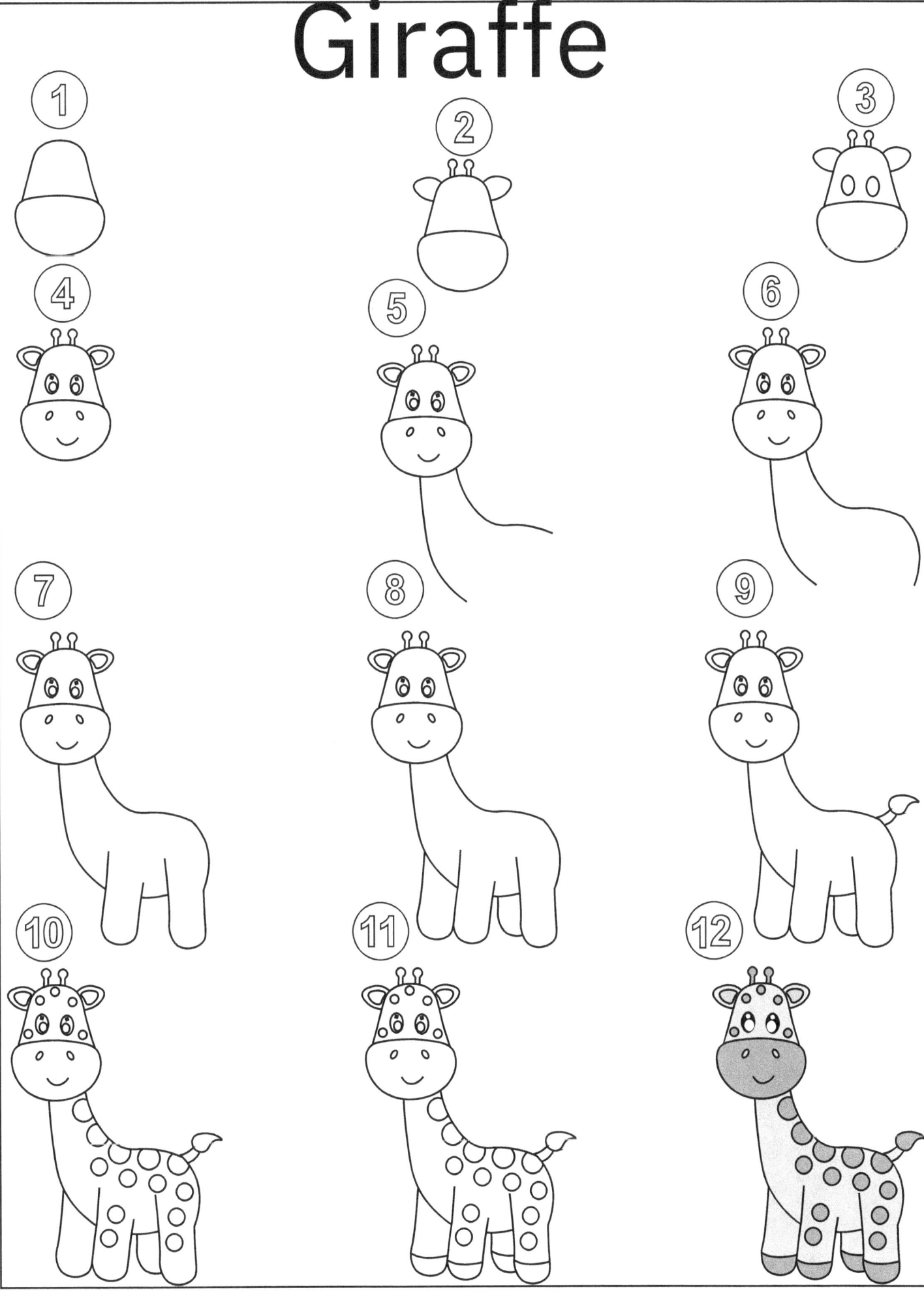

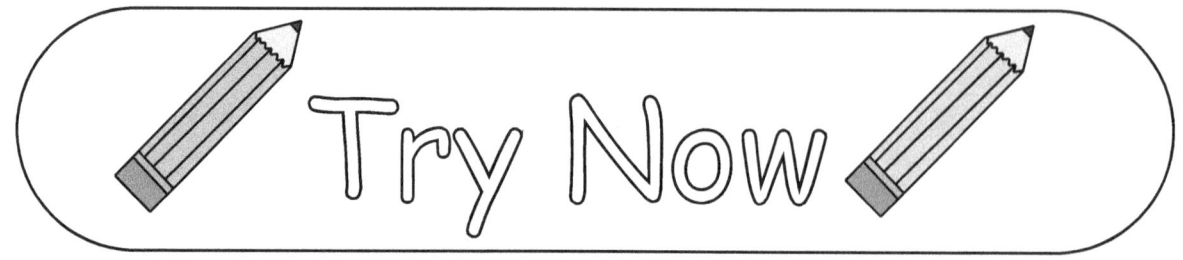

Deer

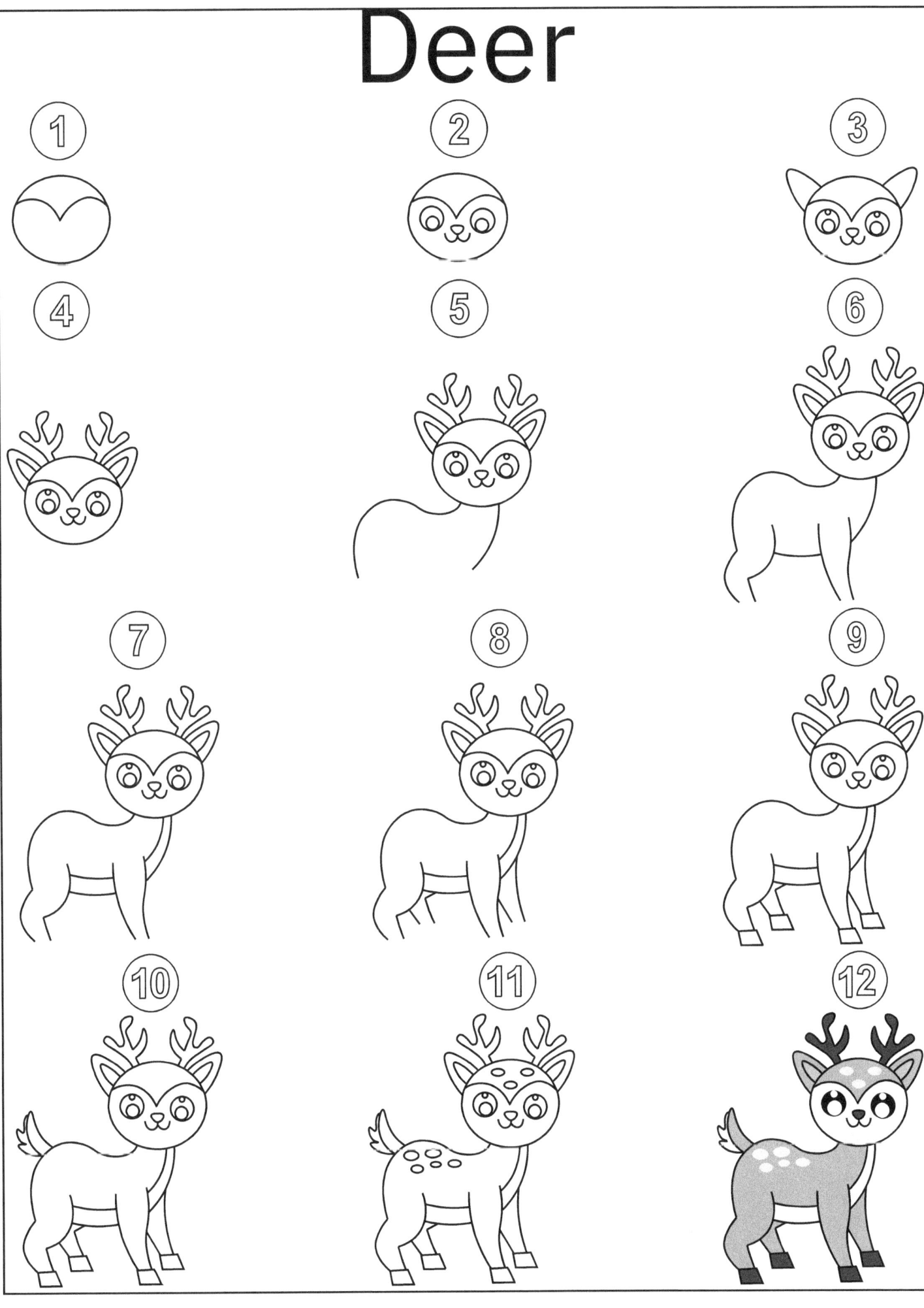

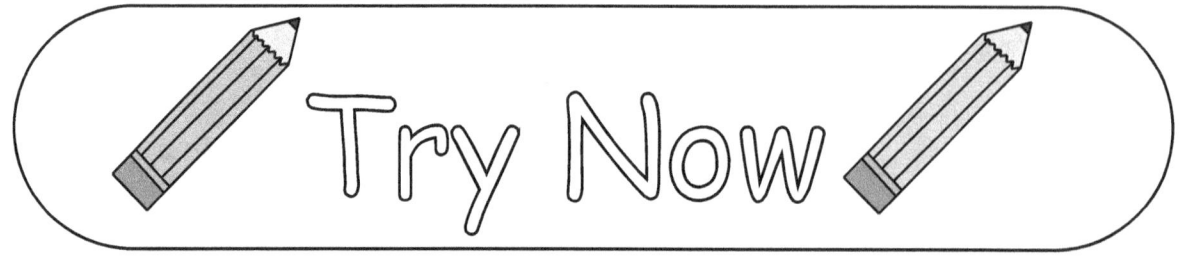

Zebra

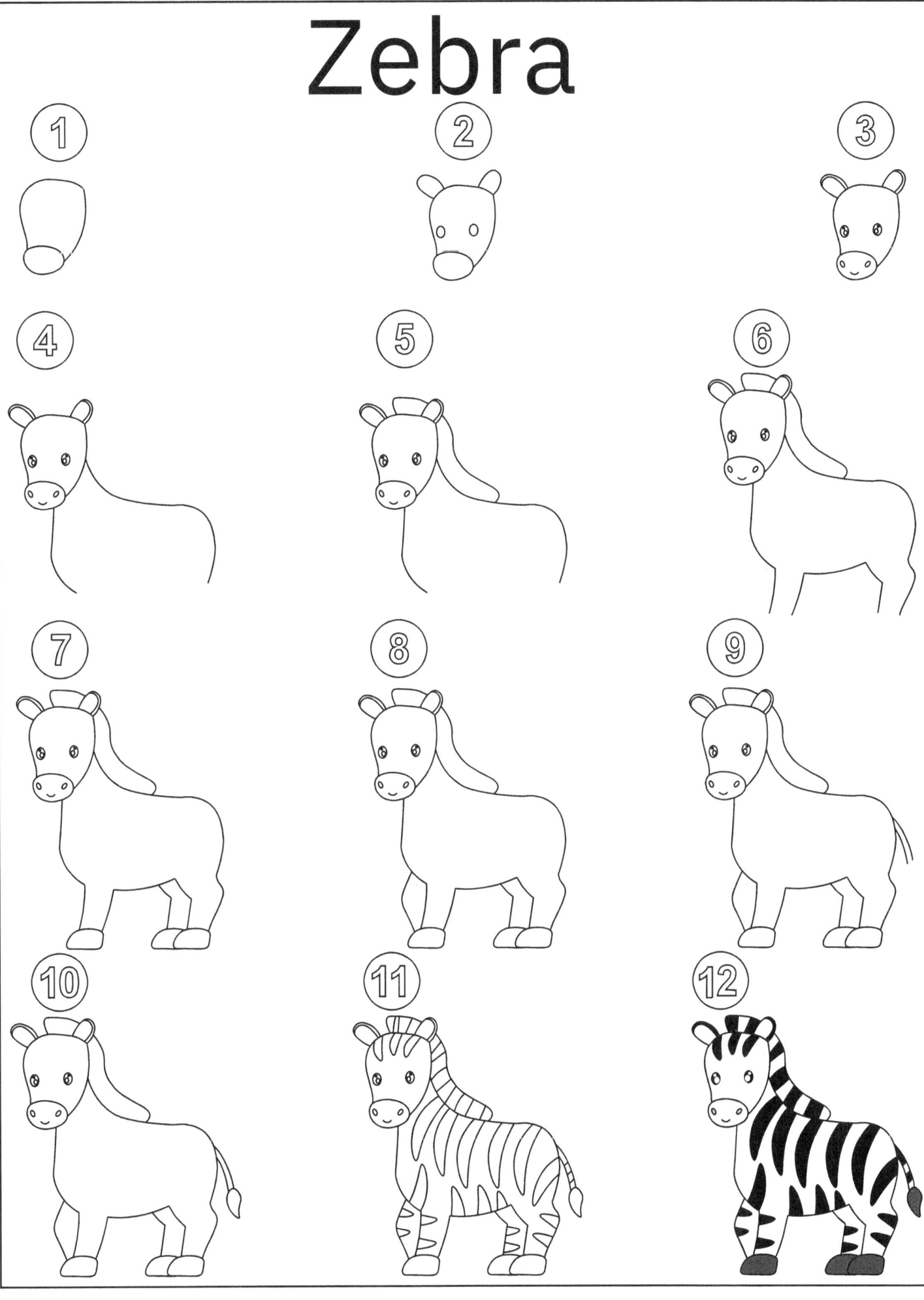

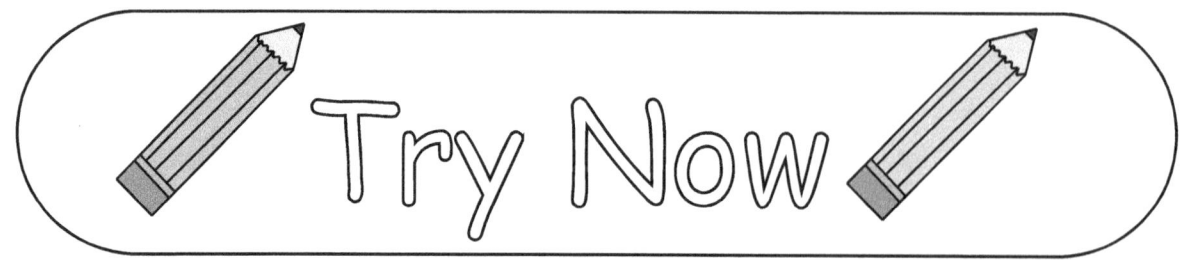

Monkey

①

②

③

④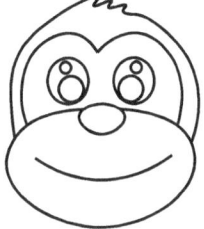

⑤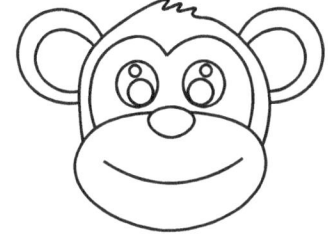

⑥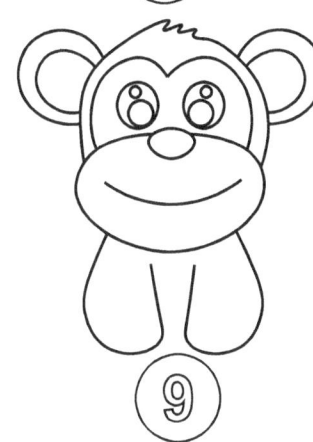

⑦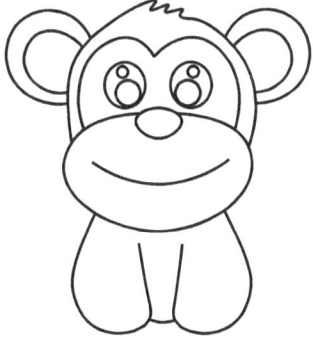

⑧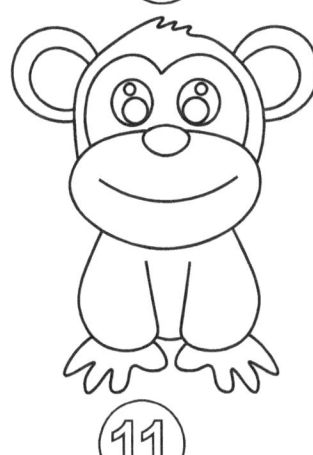

⑨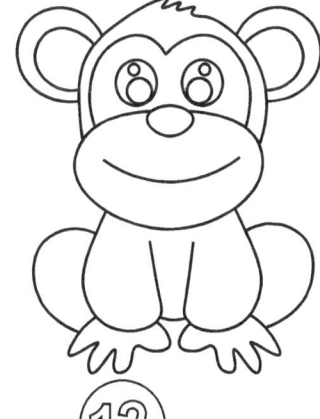

⑩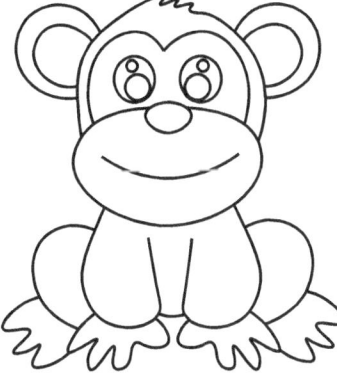

⑪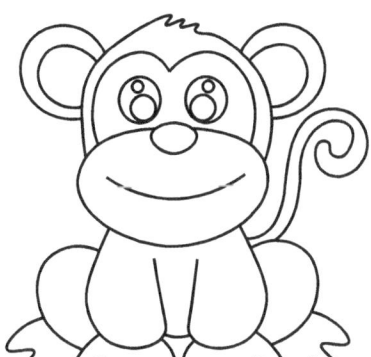

⑫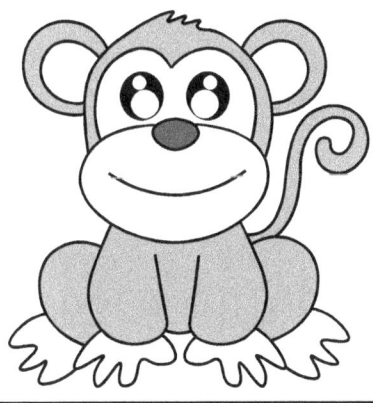

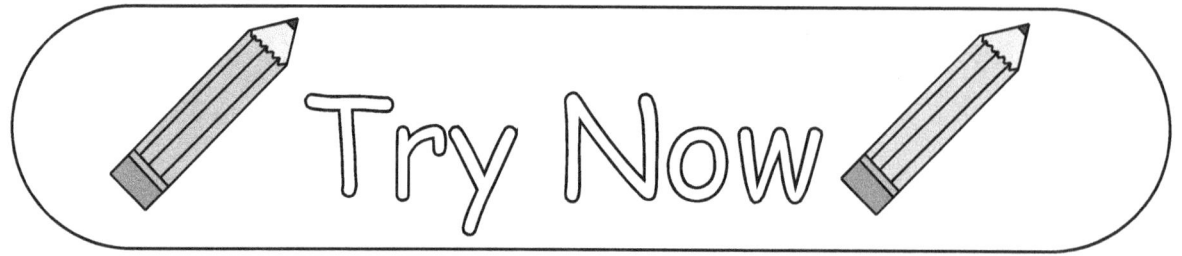
Try Now

Hippopotamus

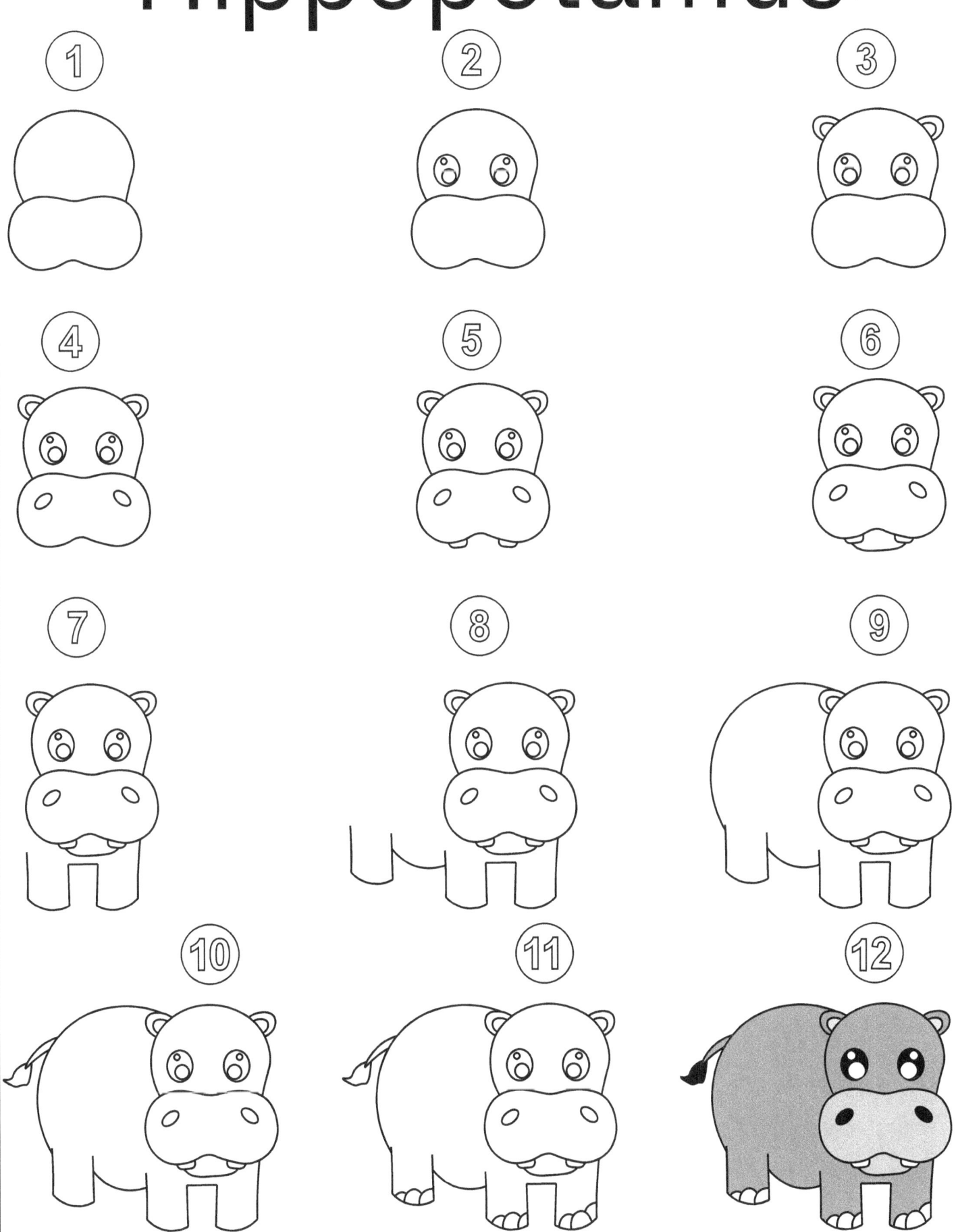

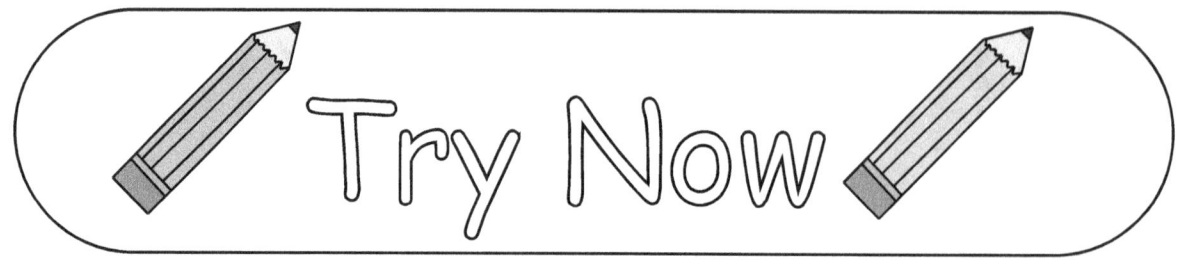

Rhinoceros

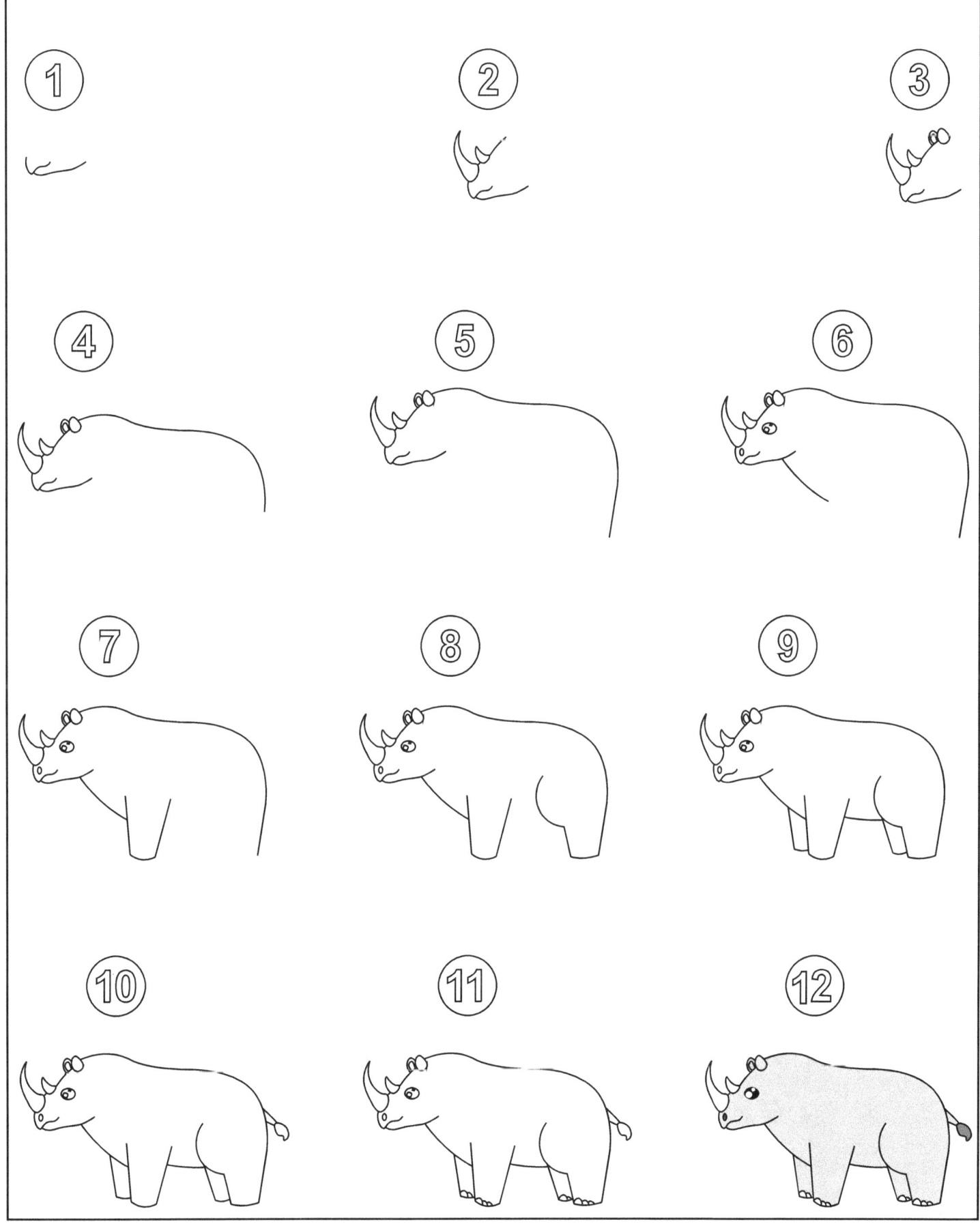

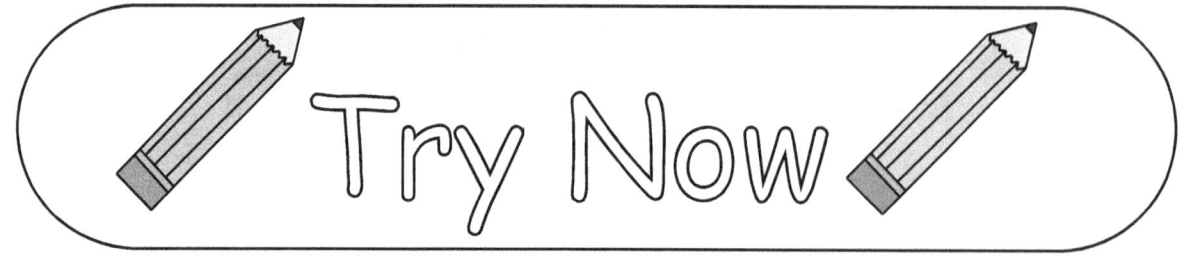

Panda

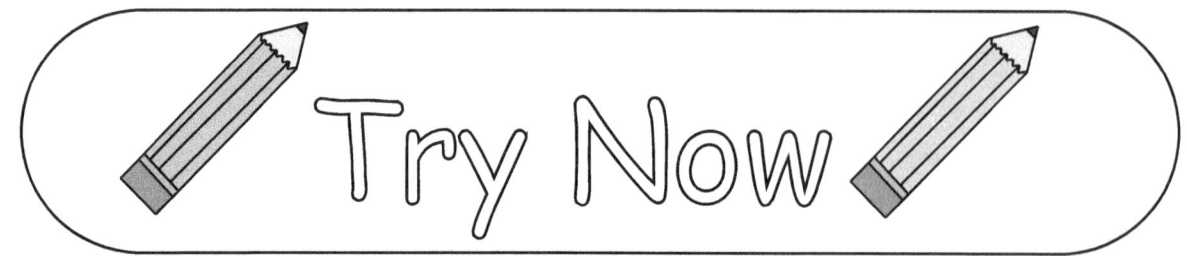

Bear

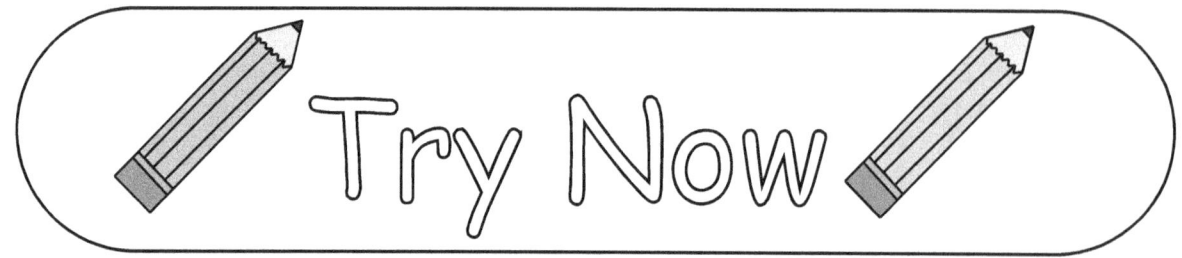

Try Now

Crocodile

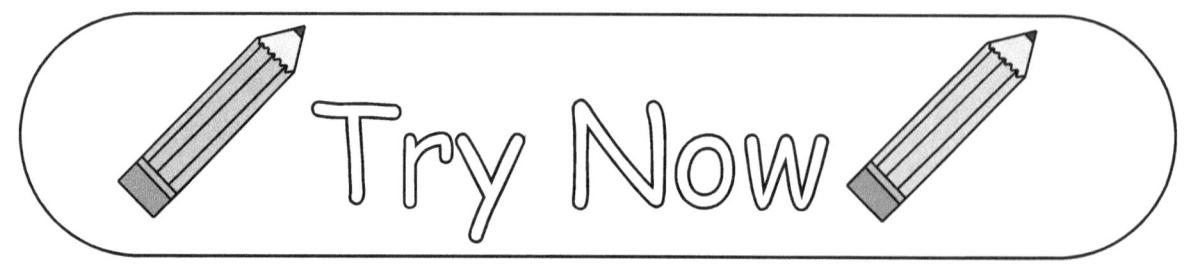

Kangaroo

1

2

3

4

5

6

7

8

9

10

11

12

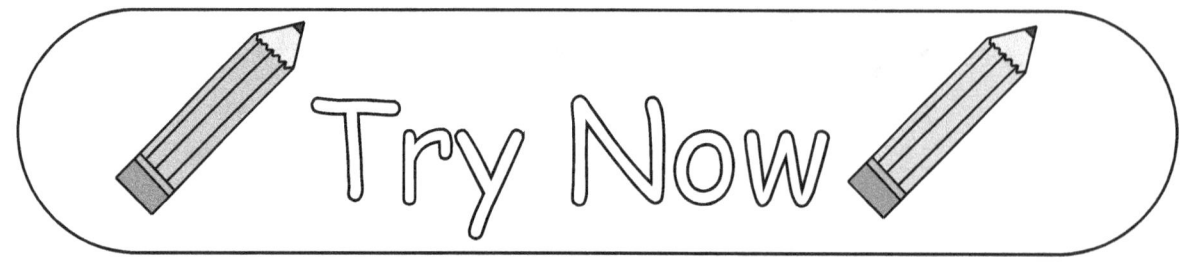

Fox

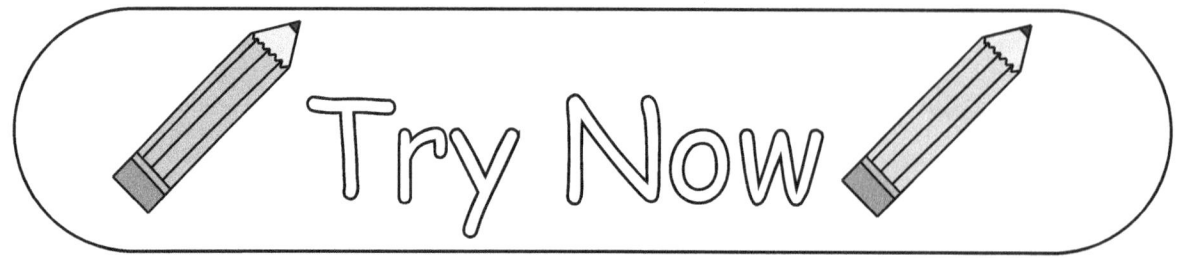

Squirrel

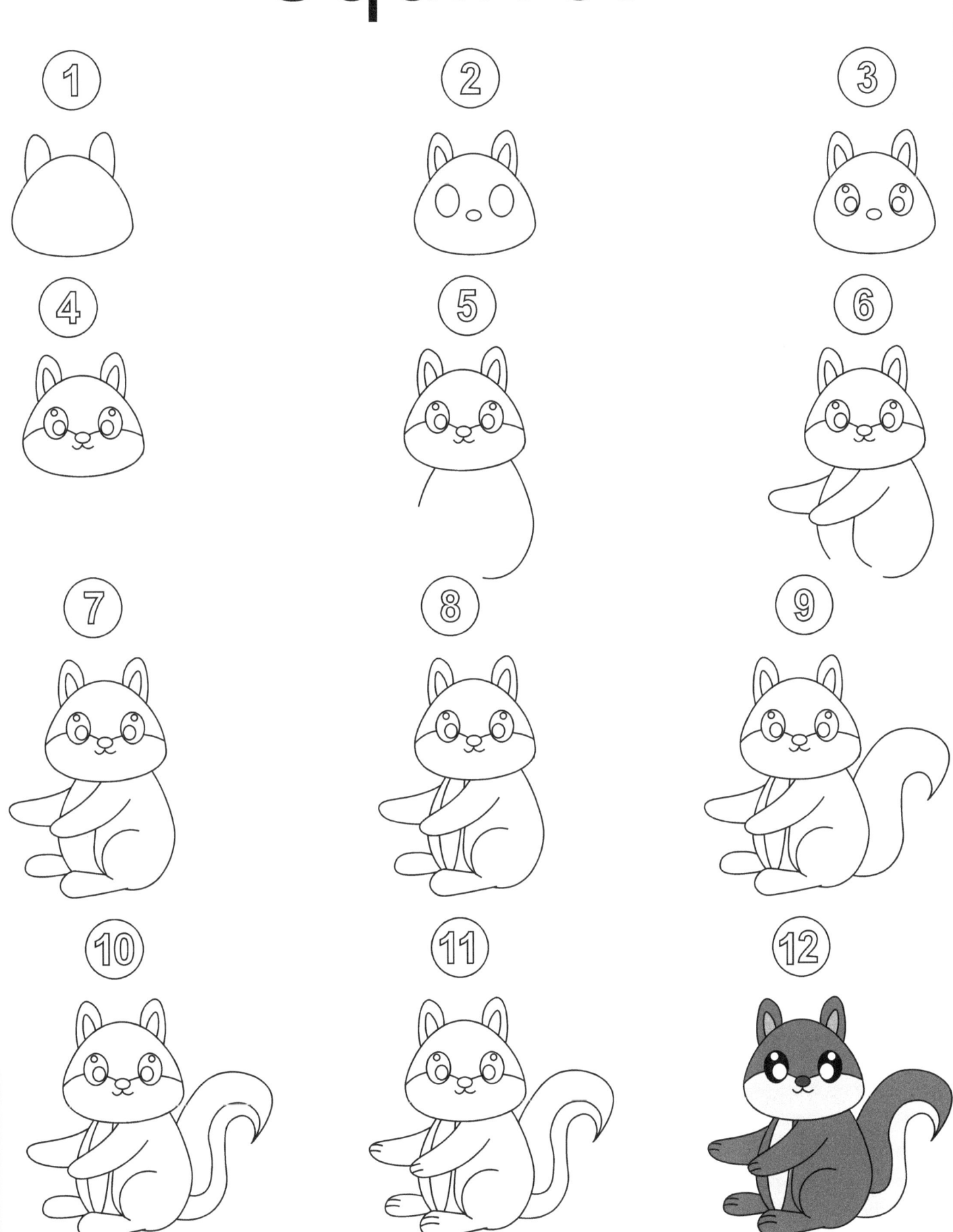

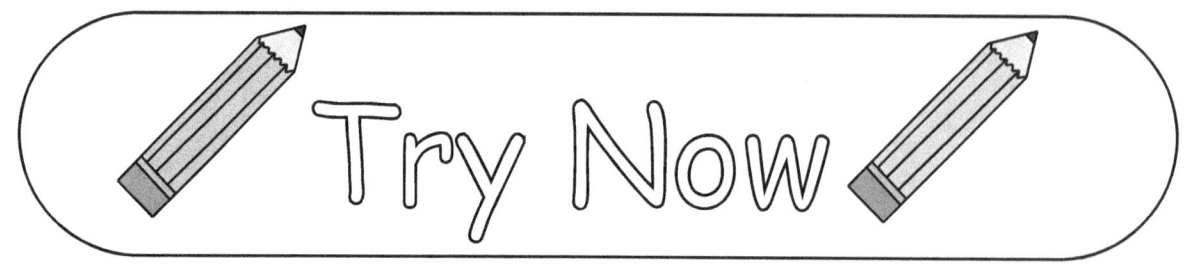

Try Now

Rabbit

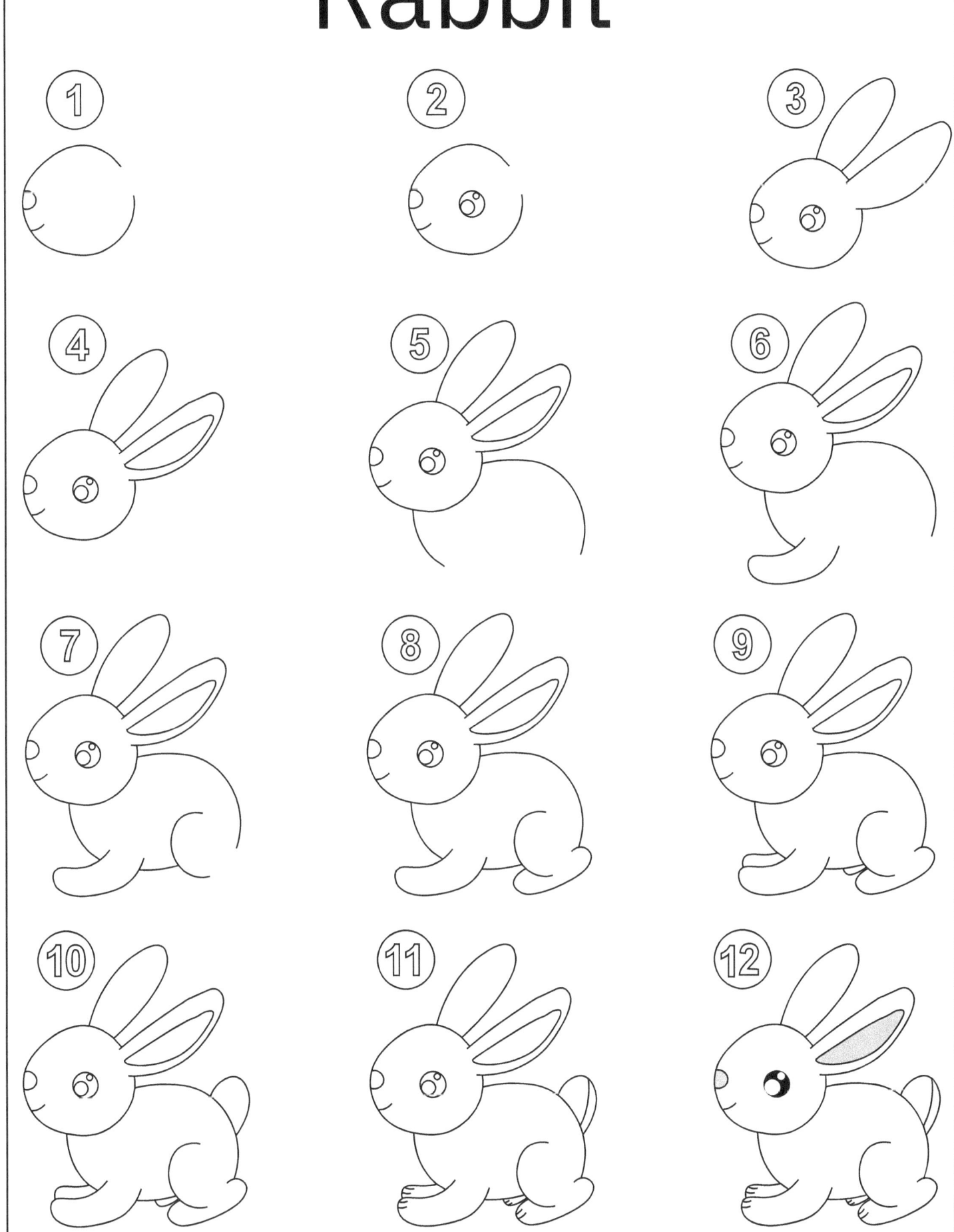

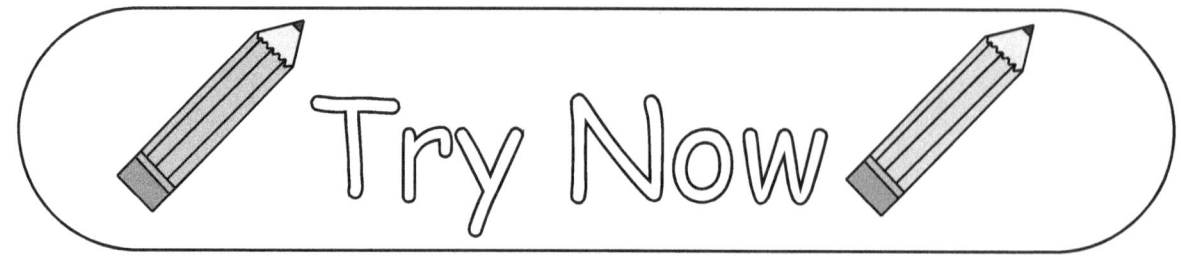

Try Now

Wolf

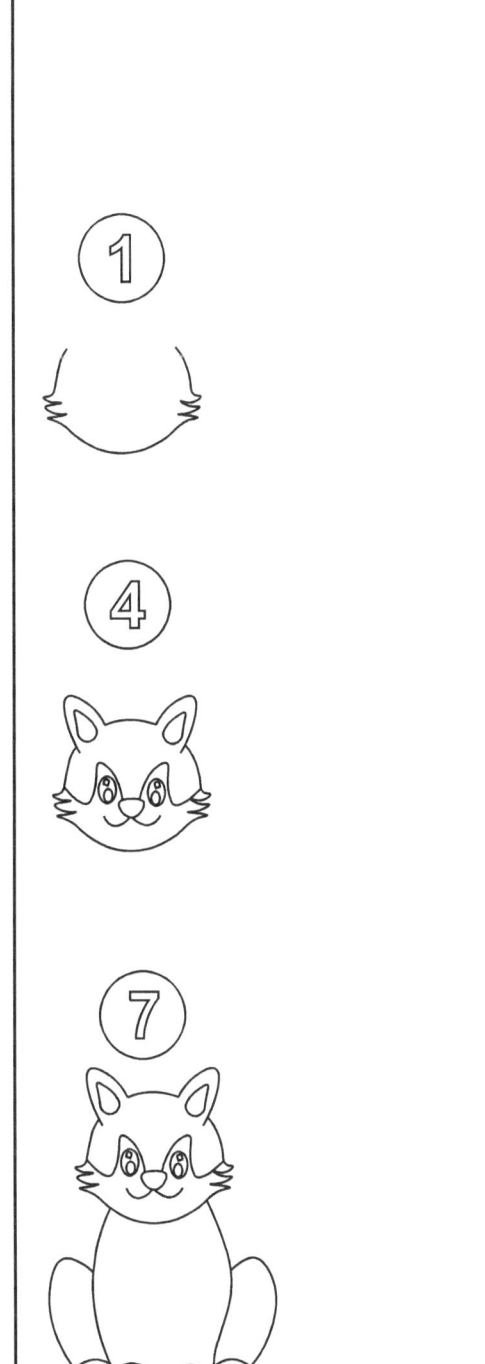

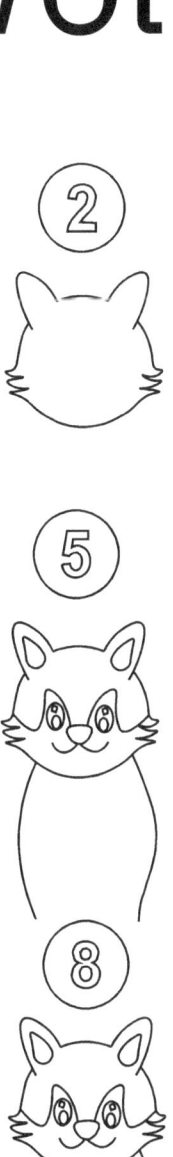
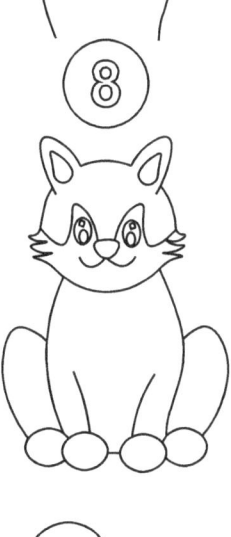
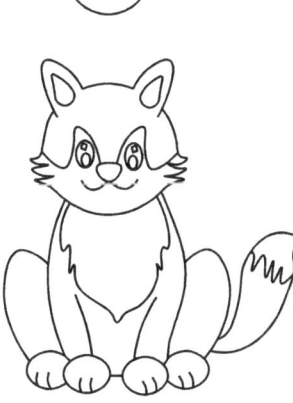
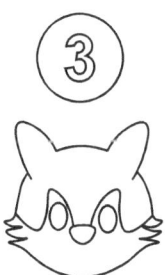
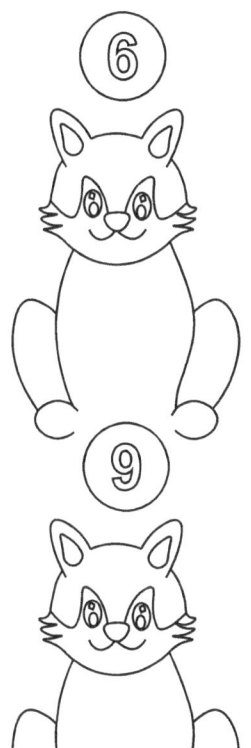
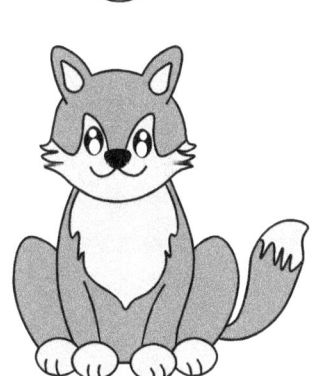

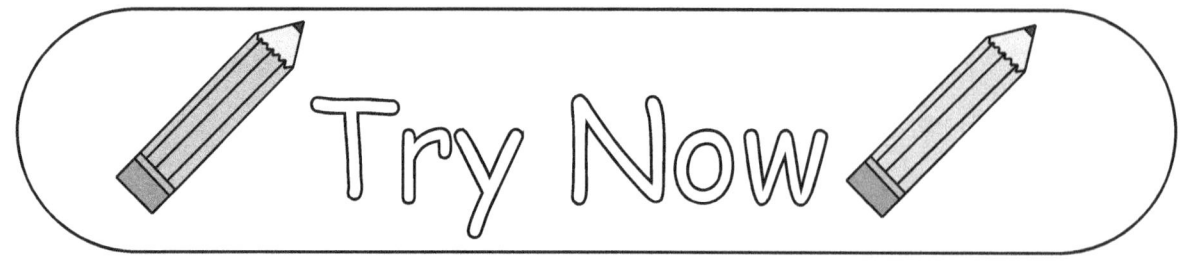

Eagle

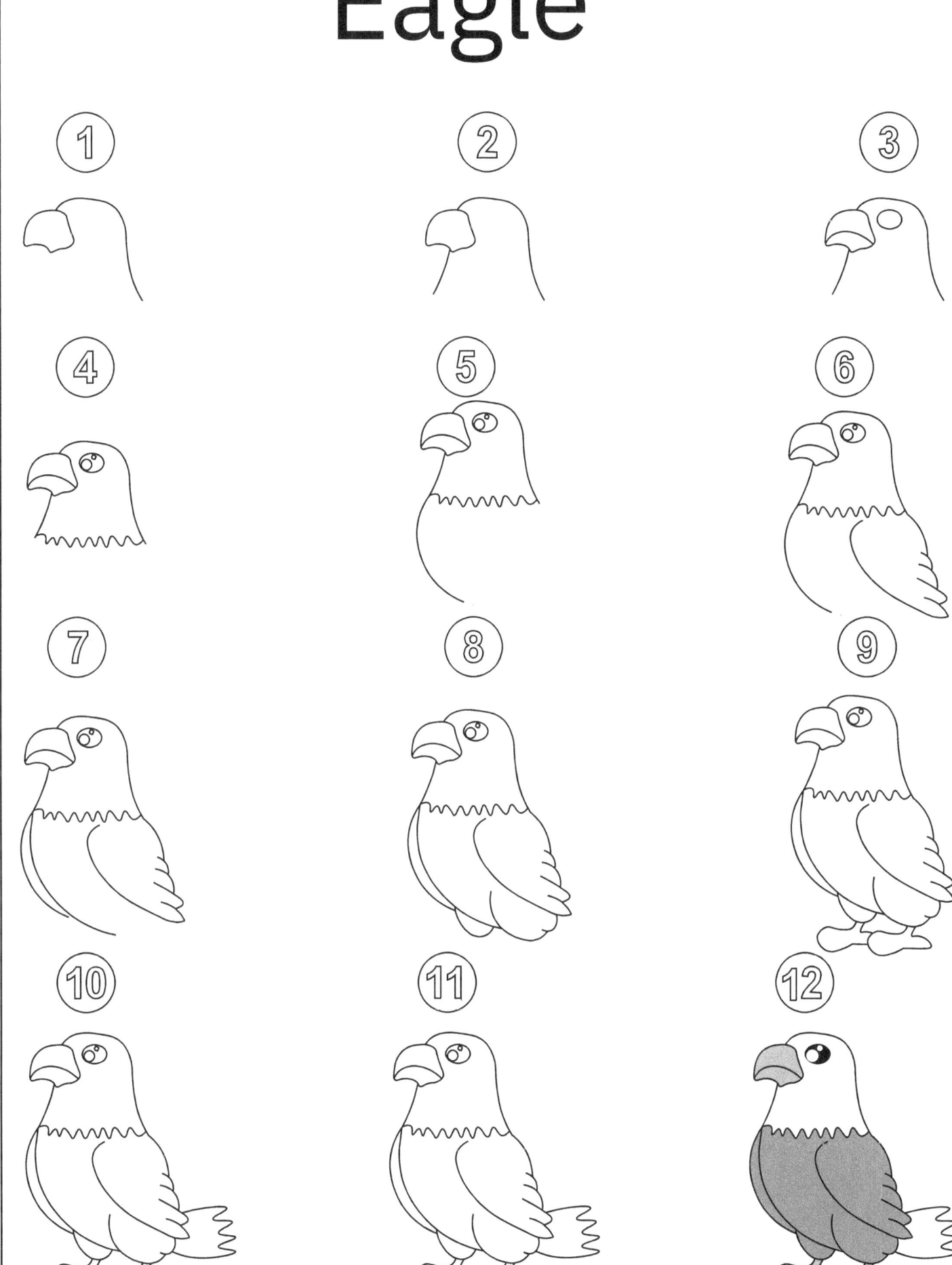

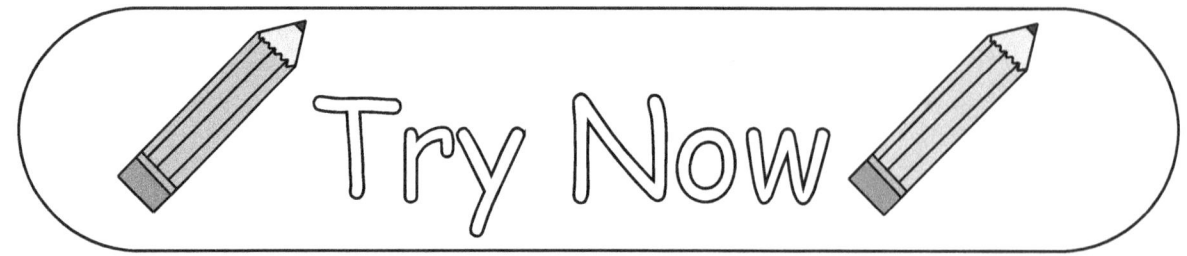

Try Now

Raccoon

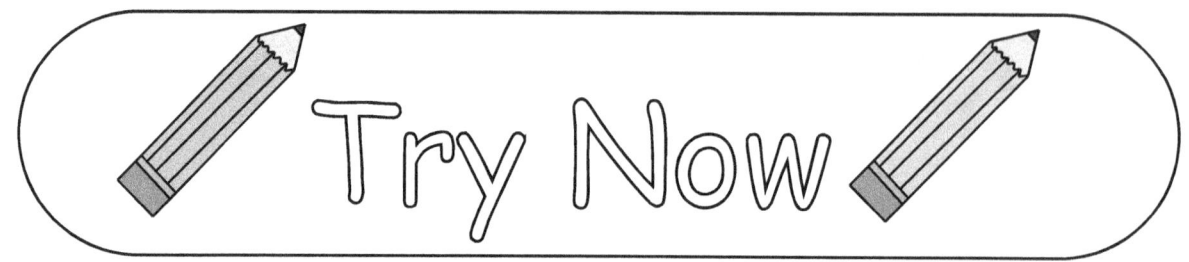

Badger

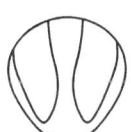

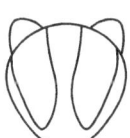

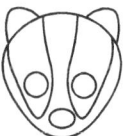

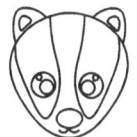

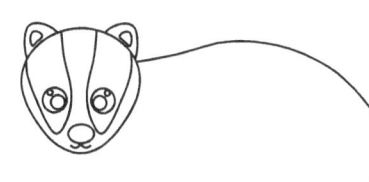

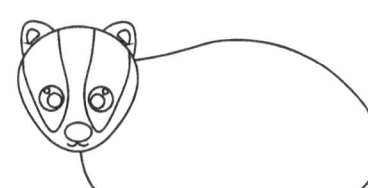

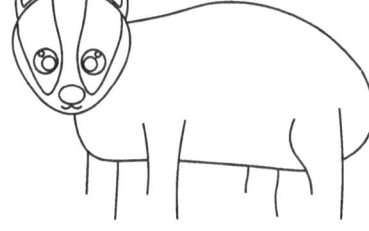

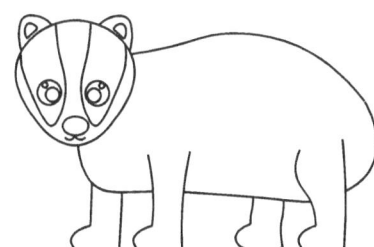

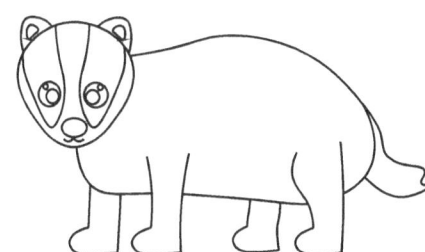

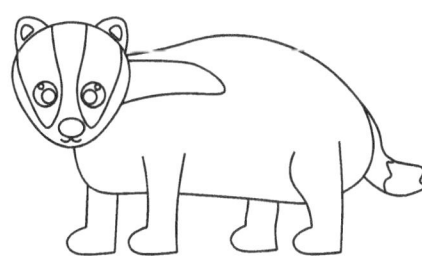

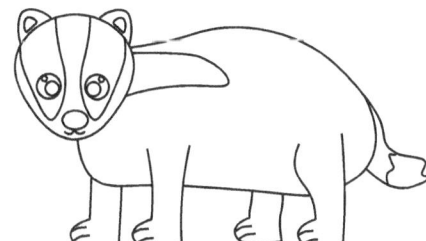

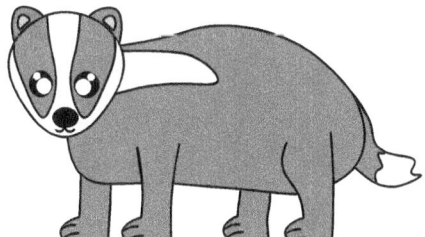

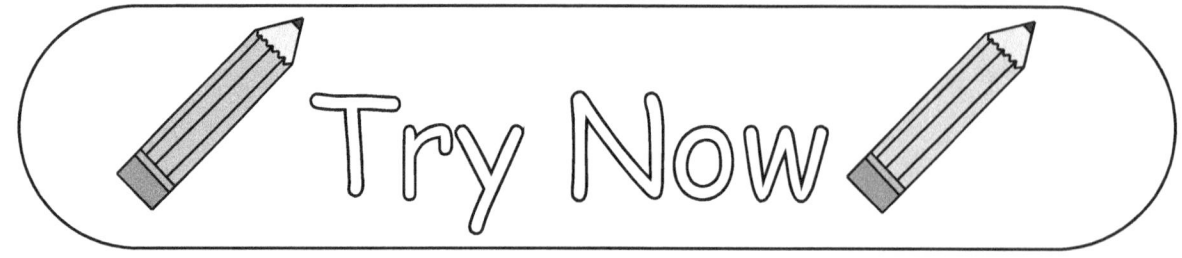

Jaguar

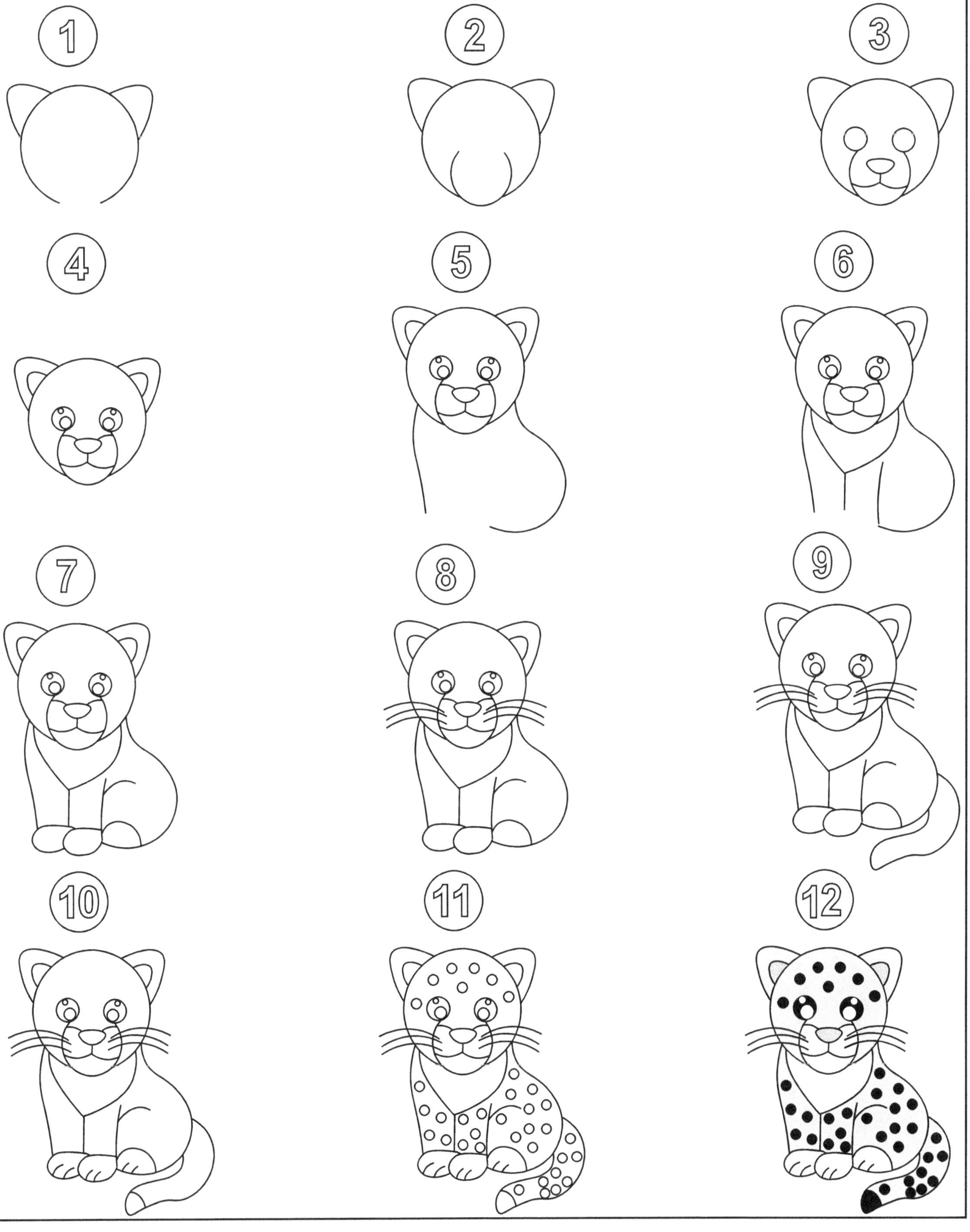

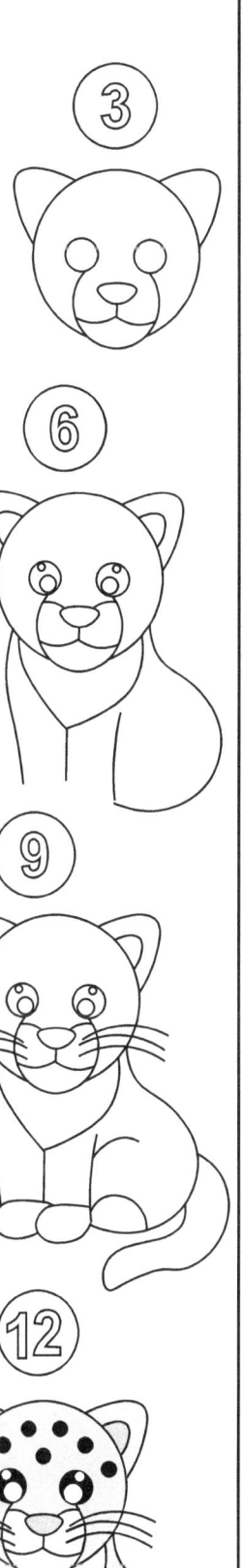

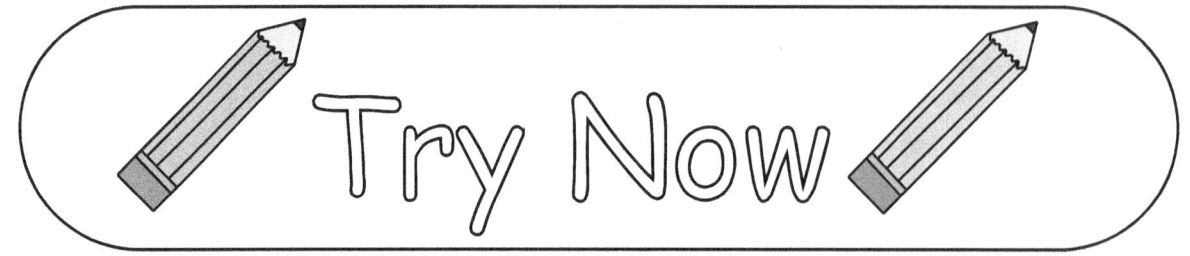

Try Now

Wombat

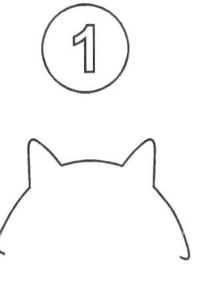

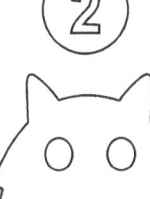

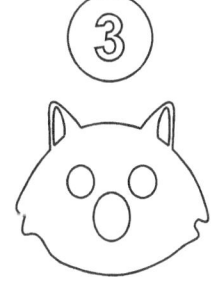

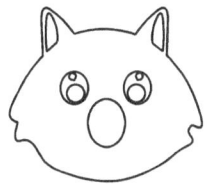

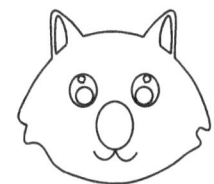

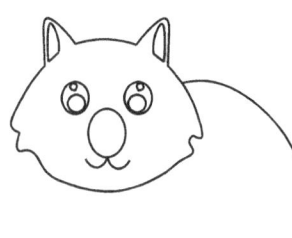

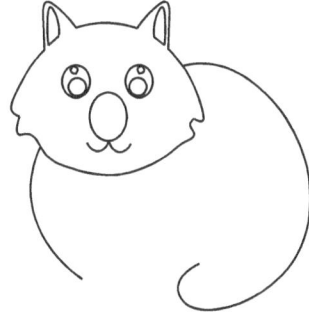

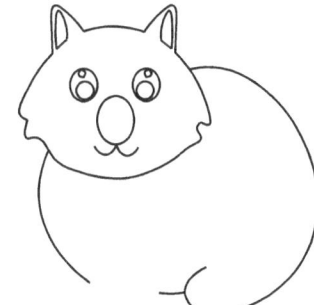

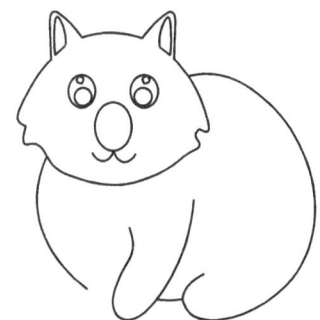

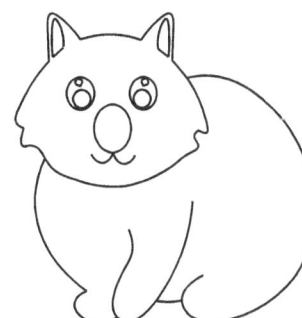

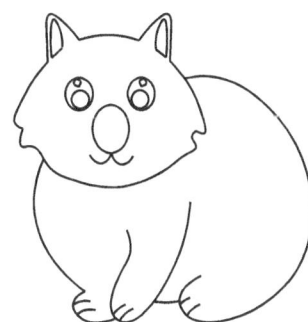

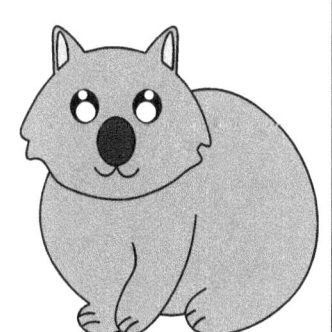

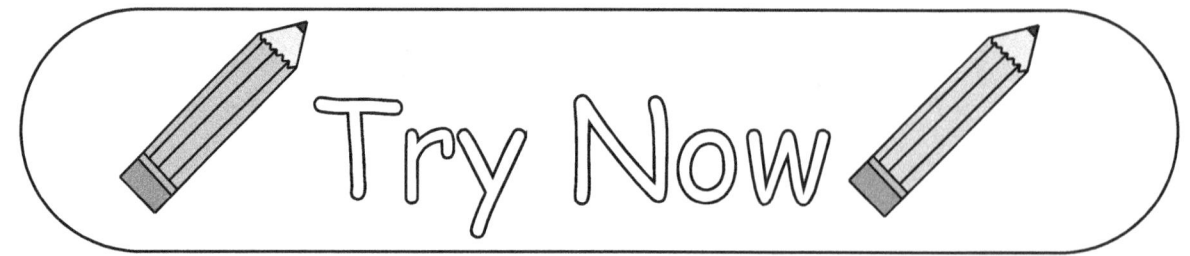

Hyena

 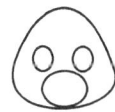

 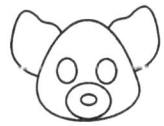

 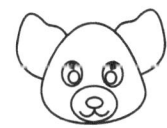

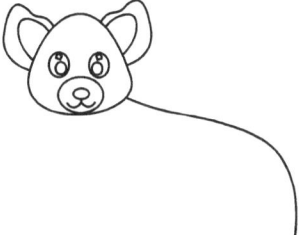

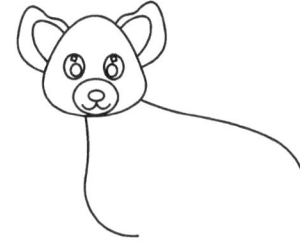

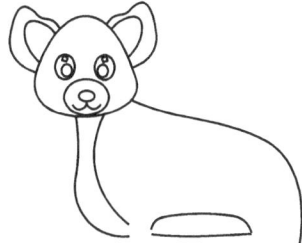

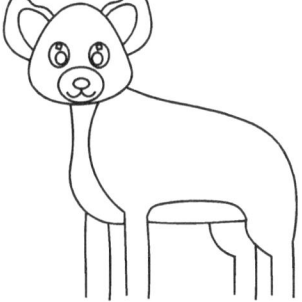

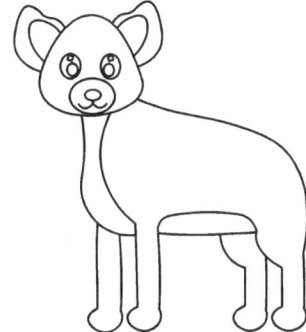

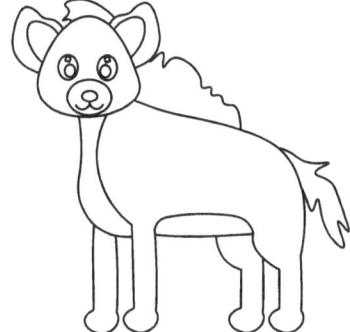

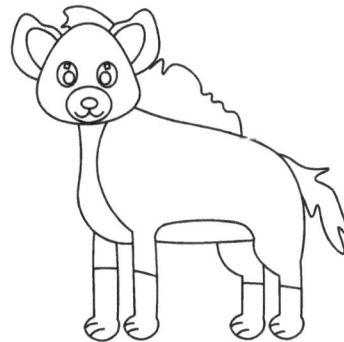

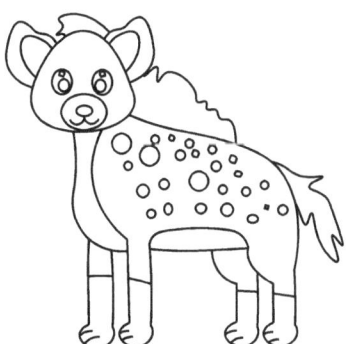

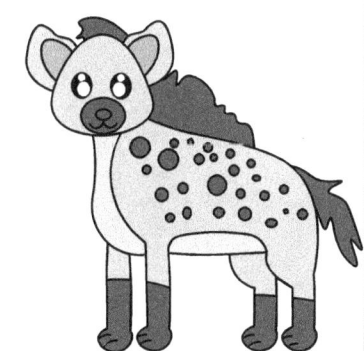

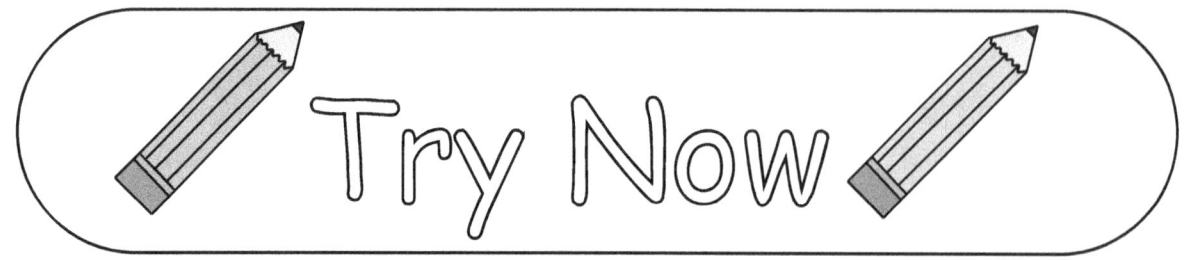

Hedgehog

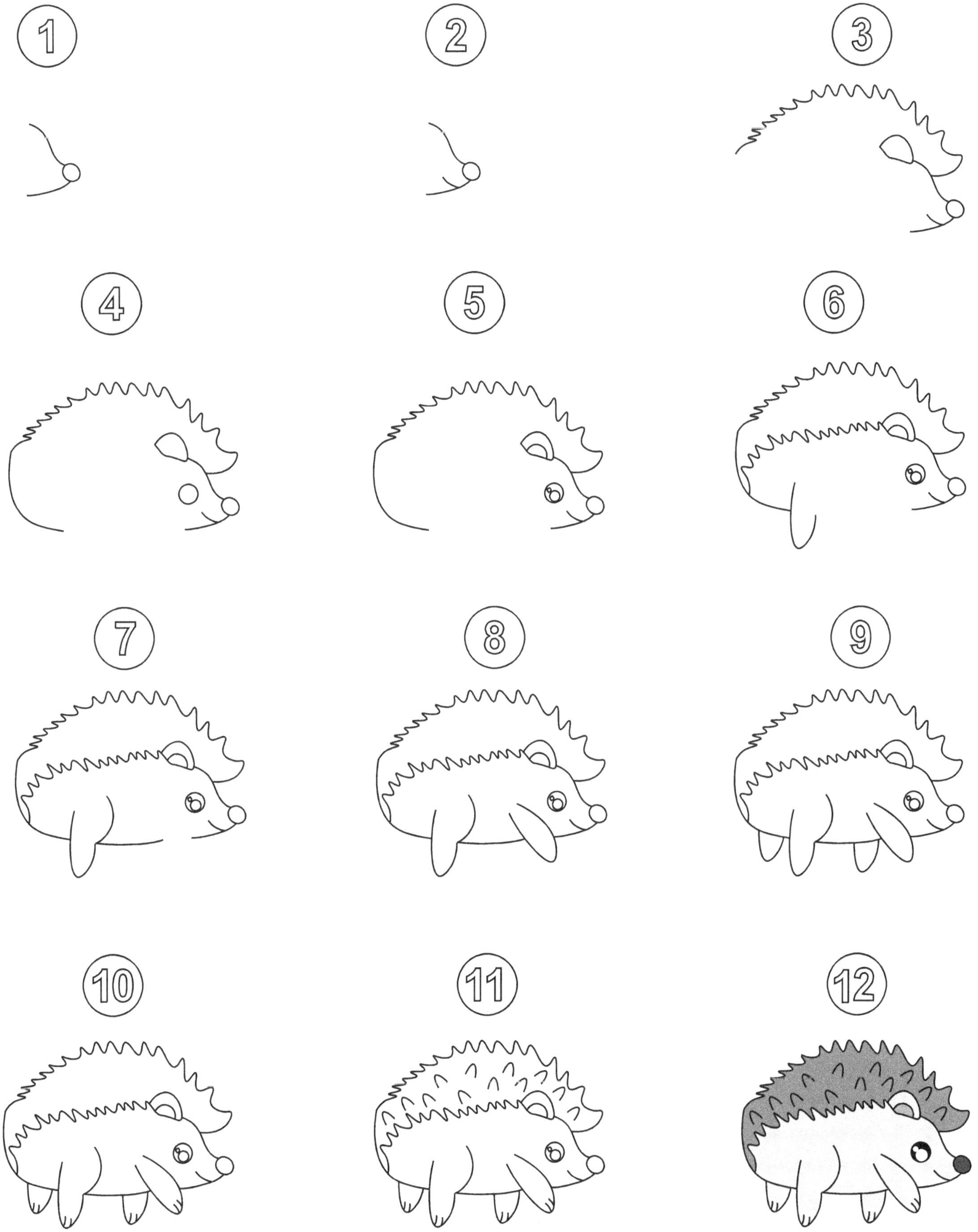

① ② ③

④ ⑤ ⑥

⑦ ⑧ ⑨

⑩ ⑪ ⑫

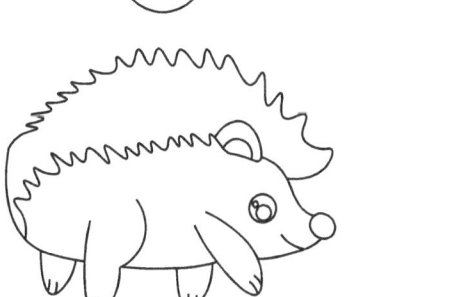
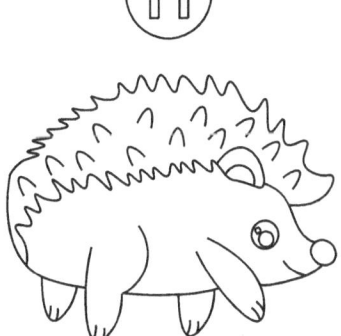
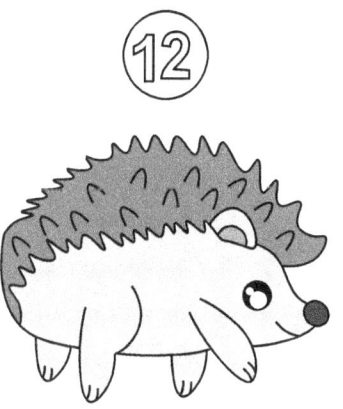

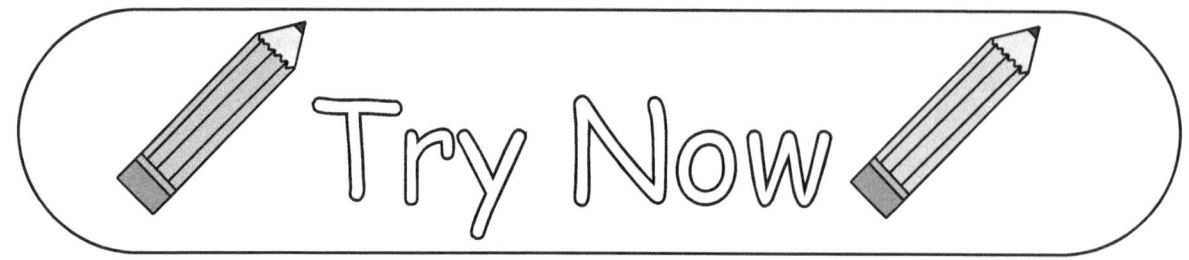

Vulture

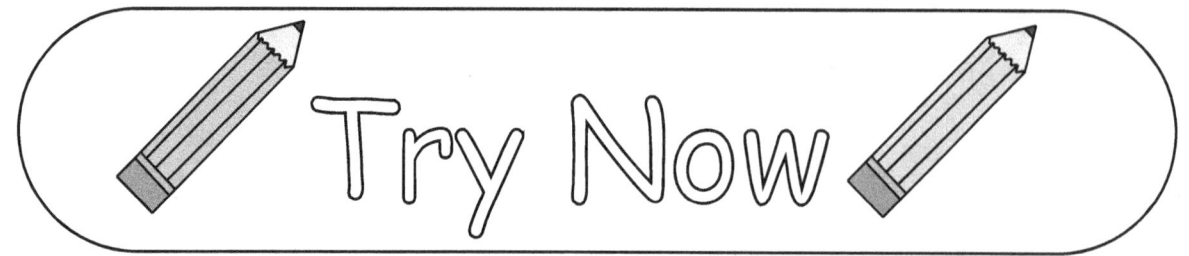

Gorilla

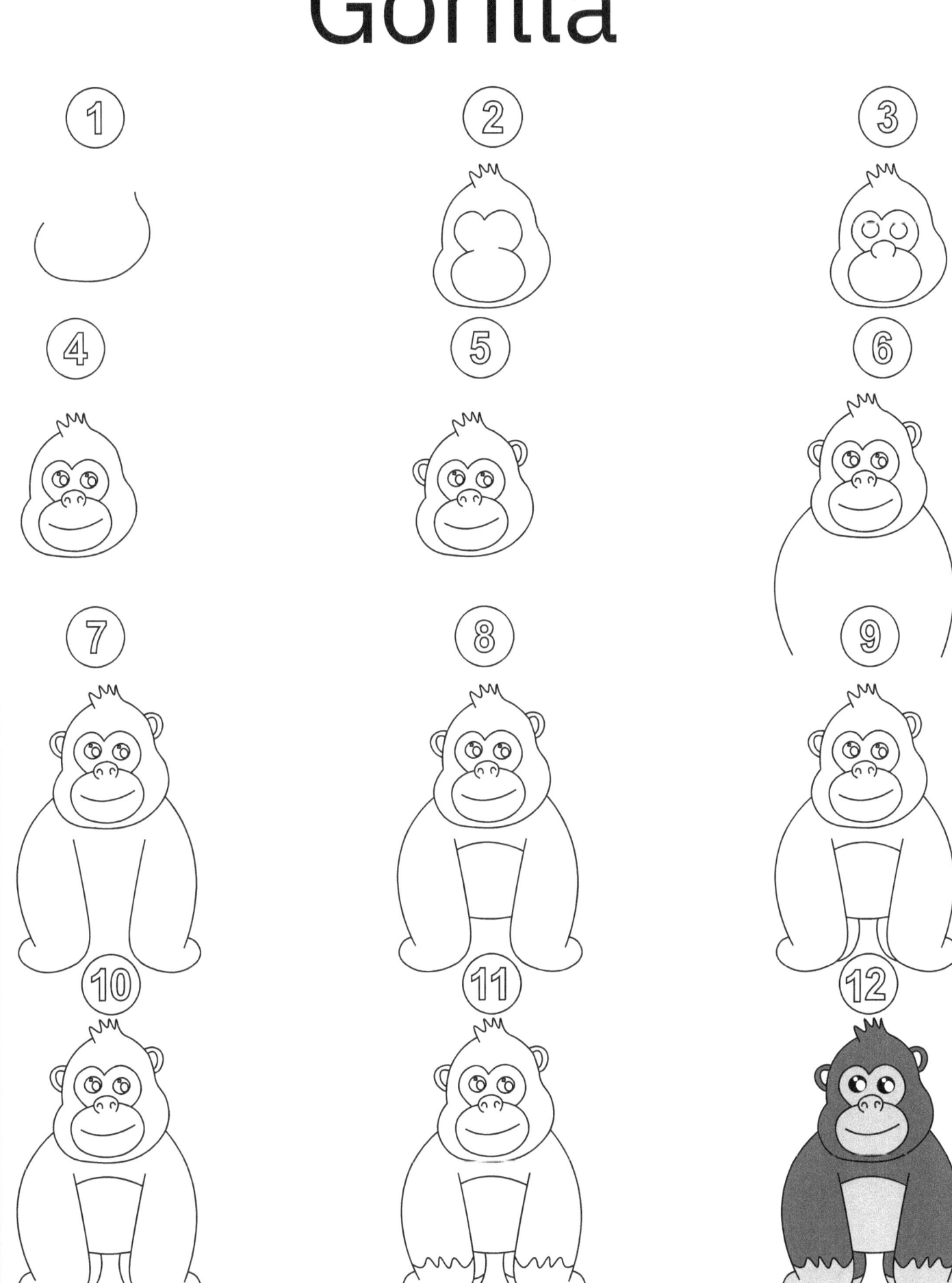

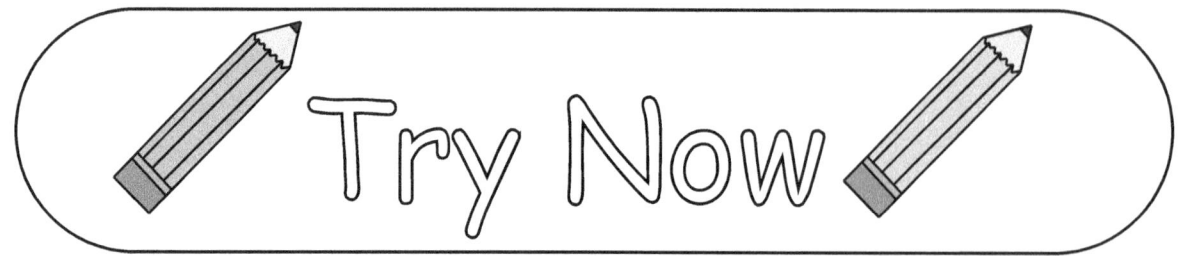

Elk

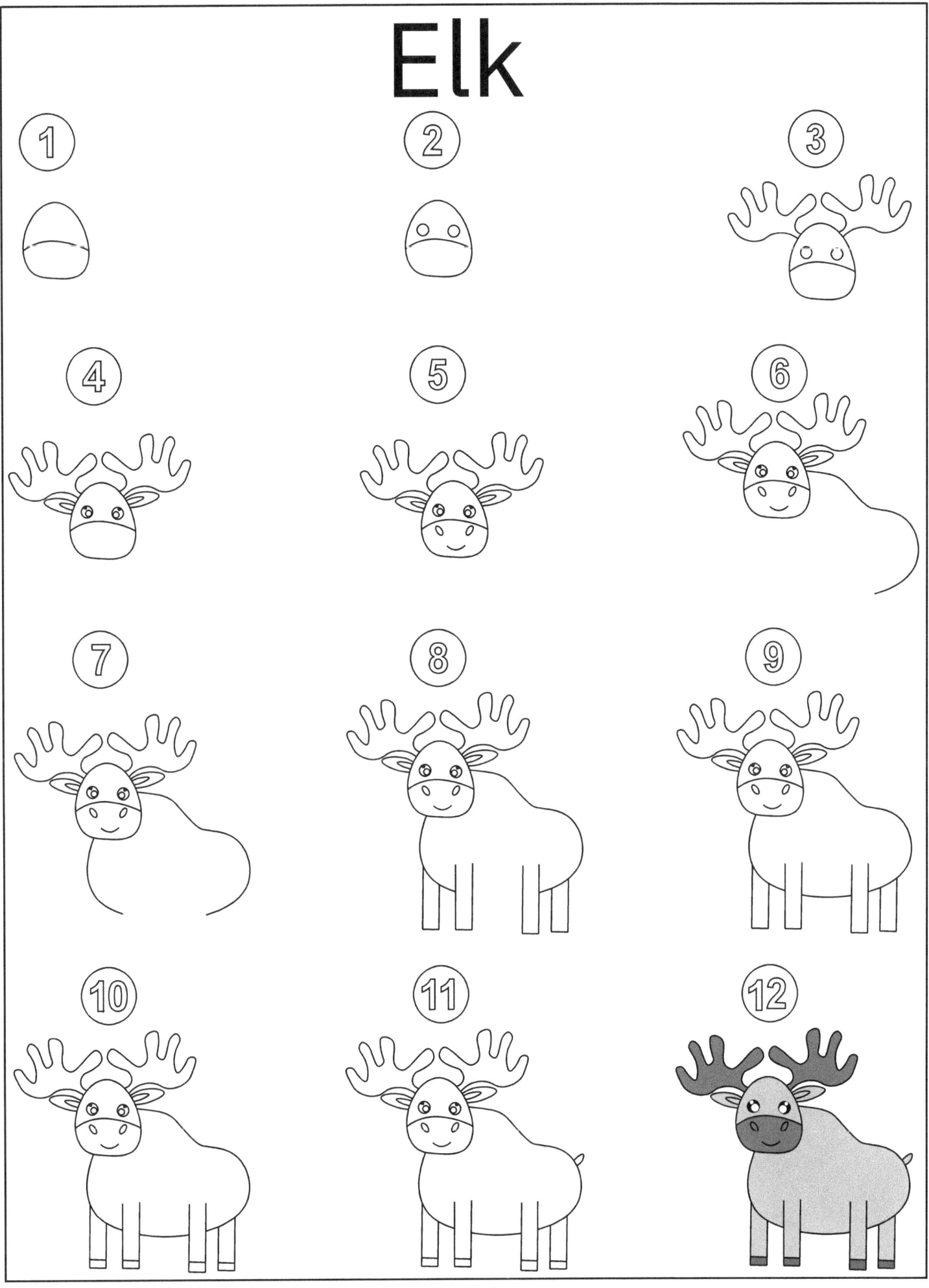

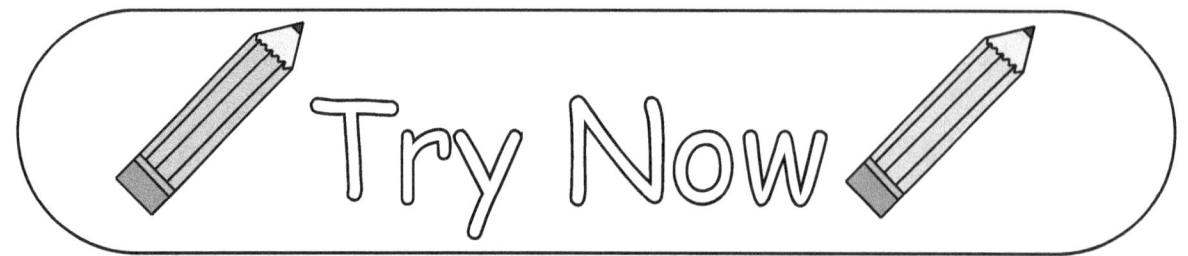

Panther

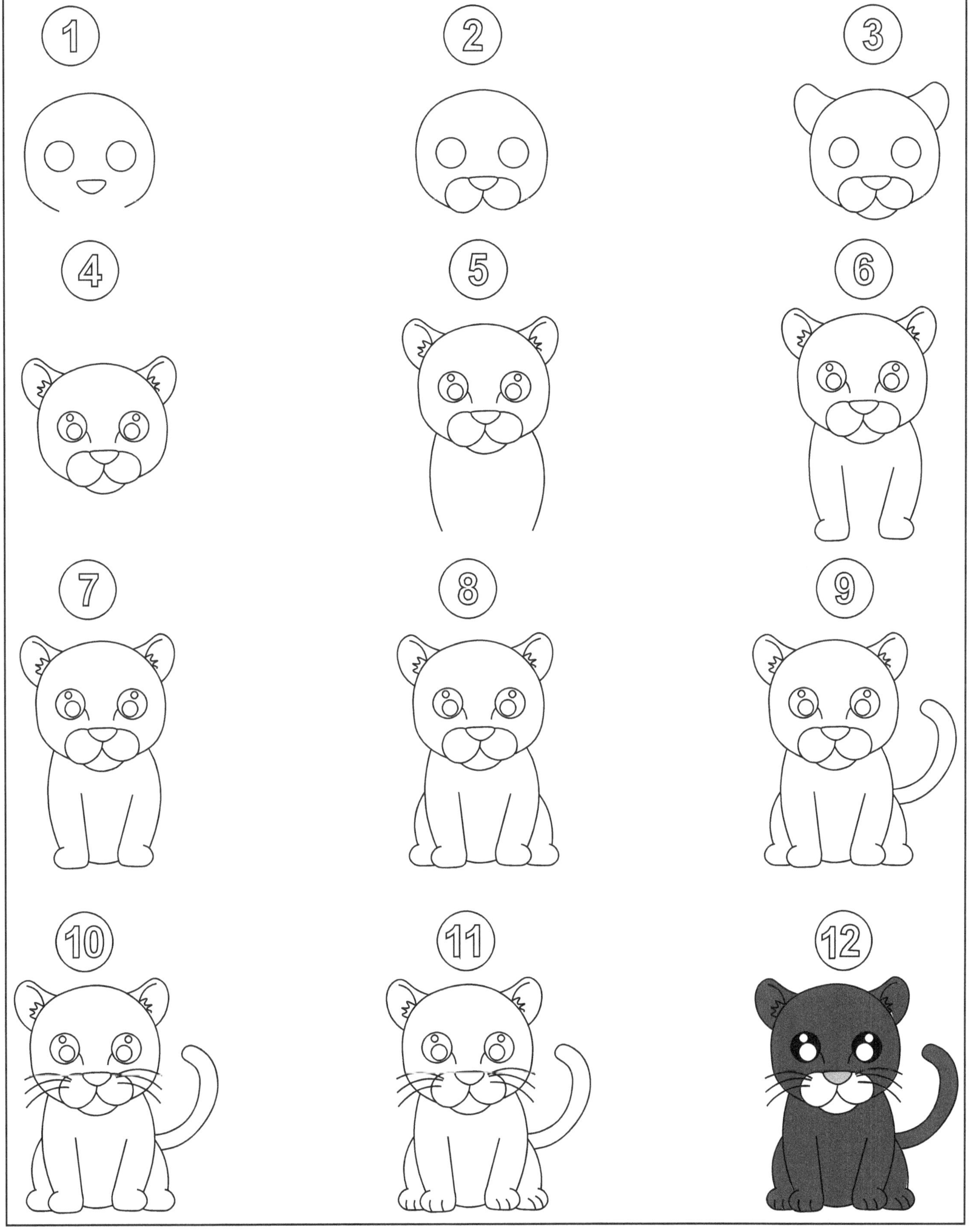

① ② ③

④ ⑤ ⑥

⑦ ⑧ ⑨

⑩ ⑪ ⑫

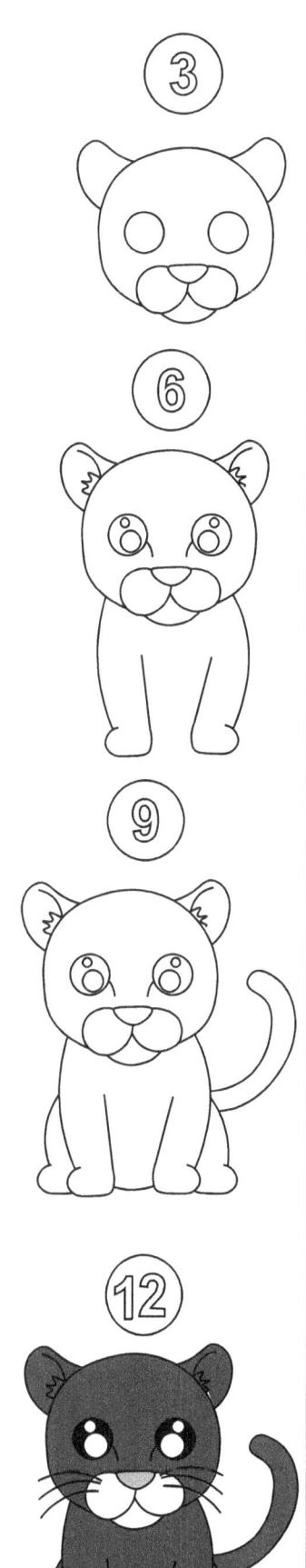

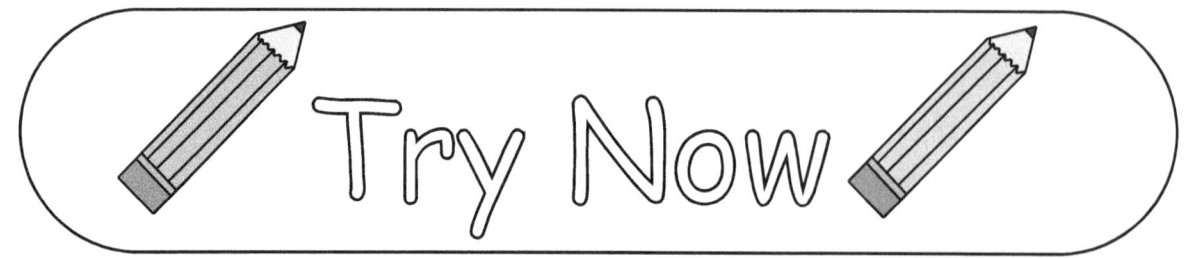

Try Now

Aardvark

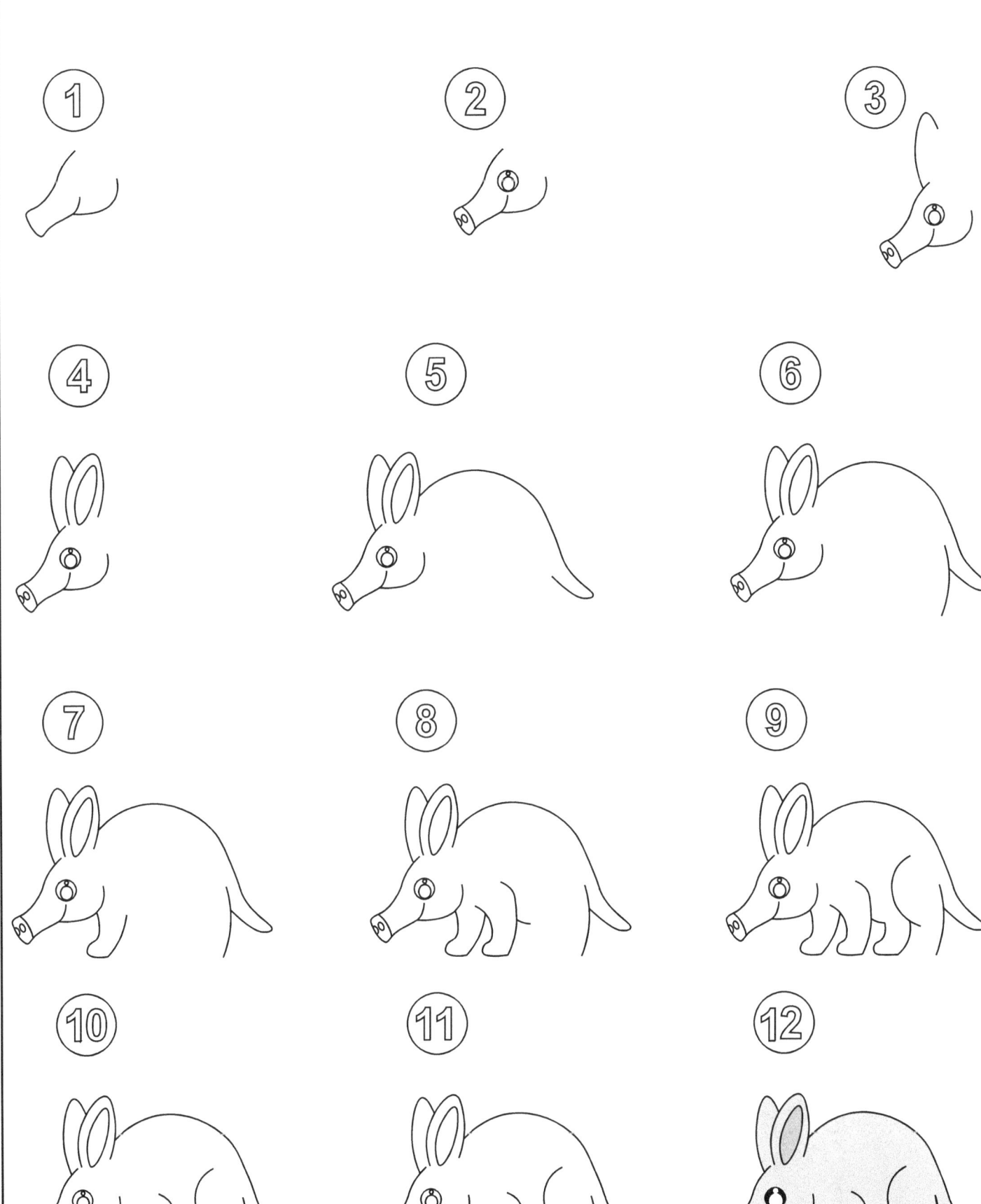

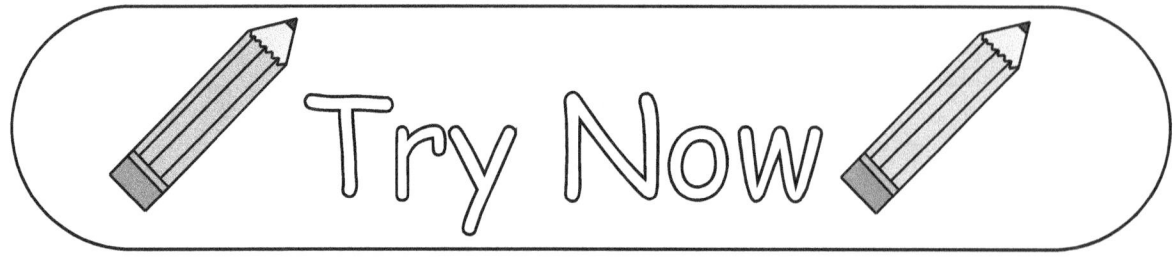

Try Now

Owl

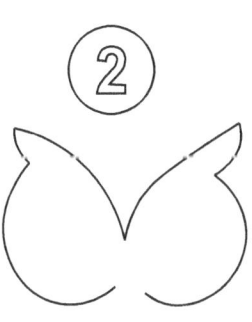
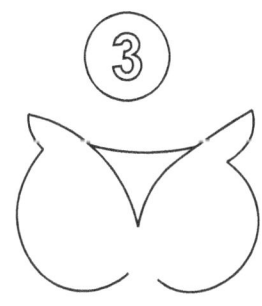
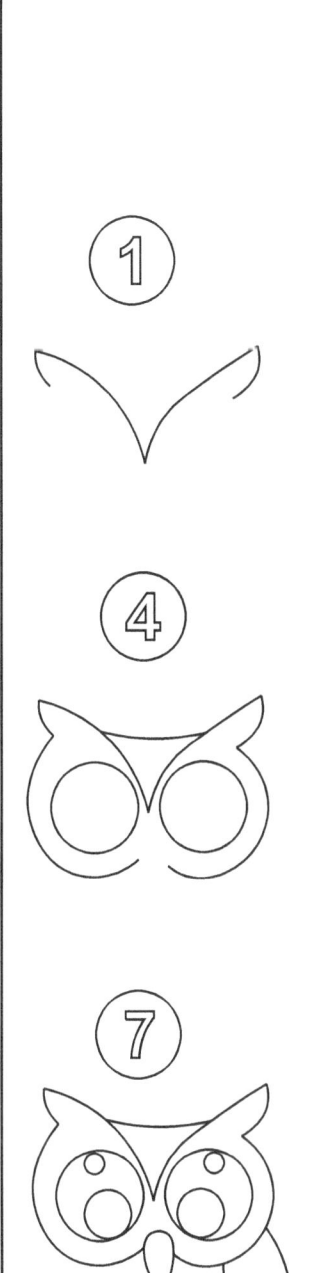
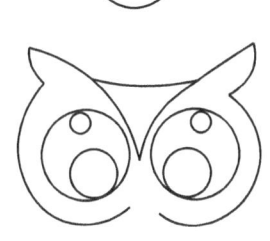
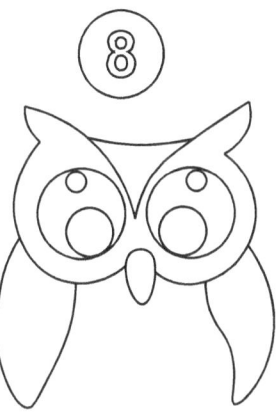
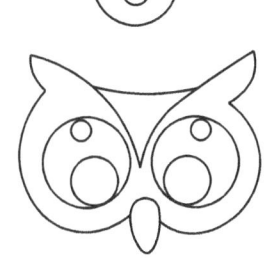
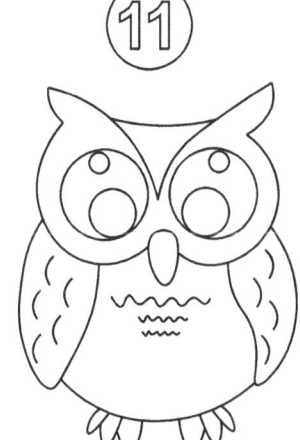
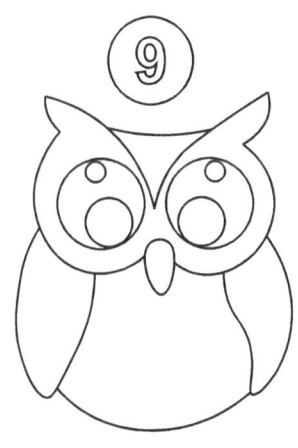
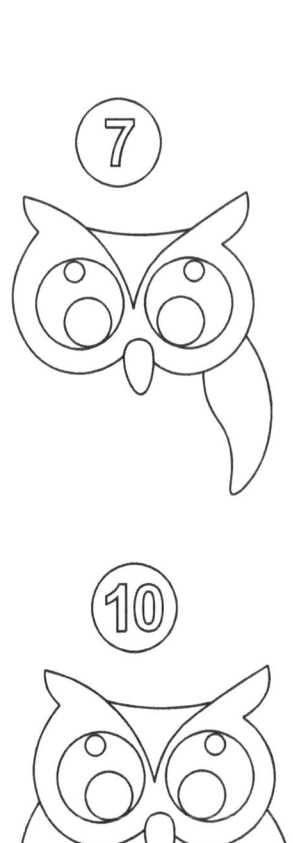
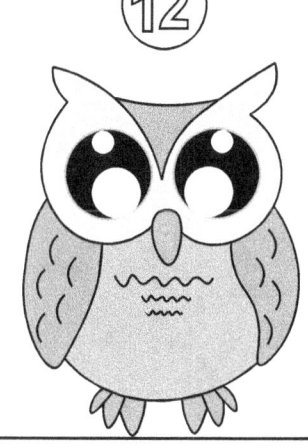

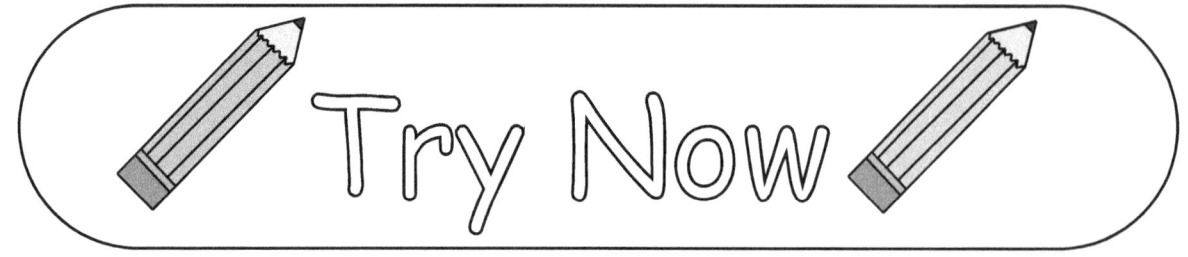

Try Now

Meerkat

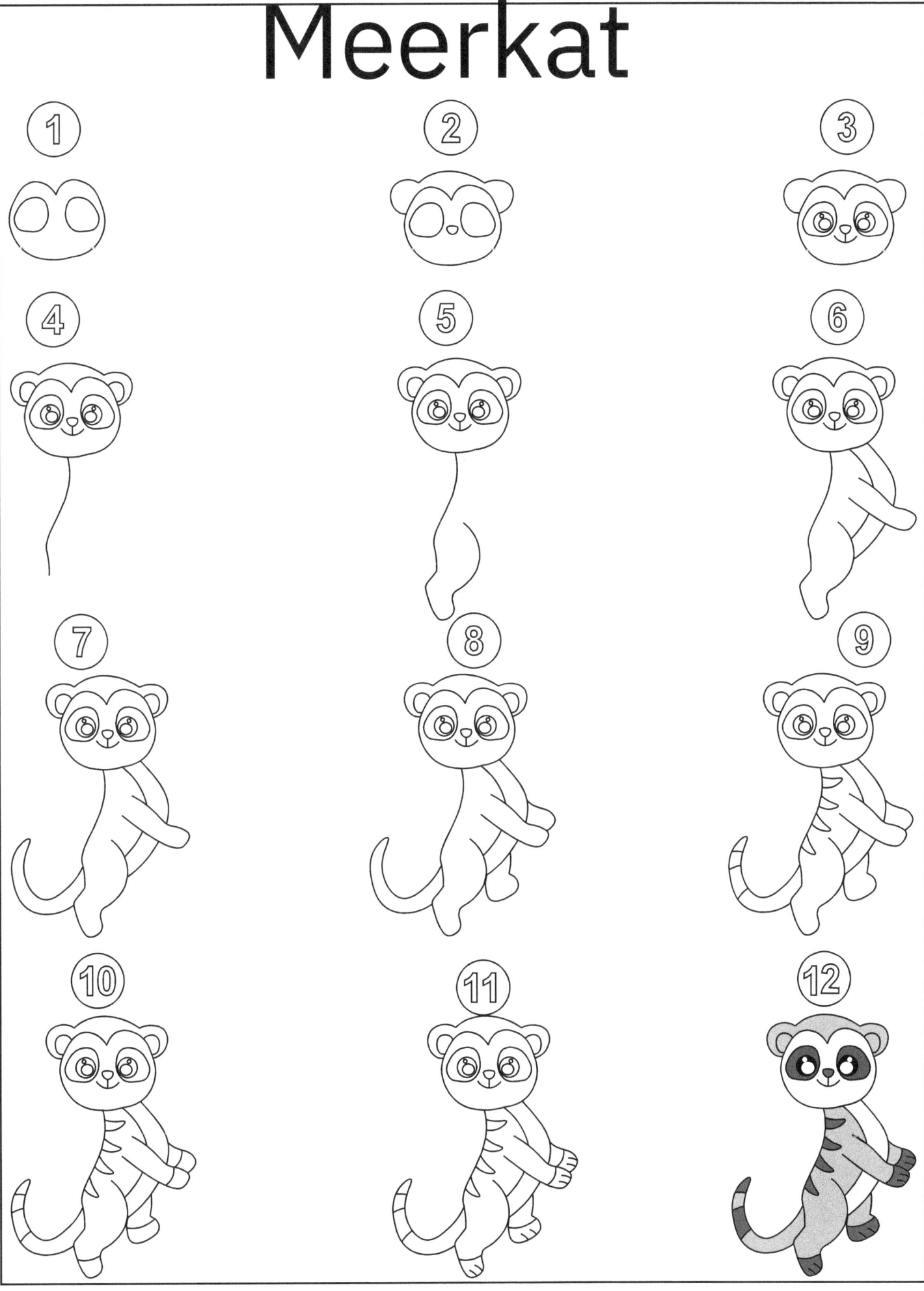

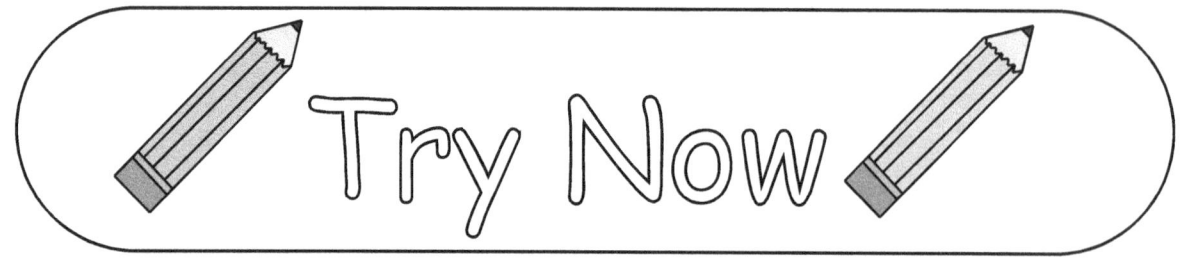

Yak

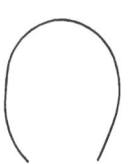

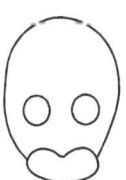

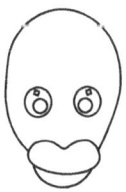

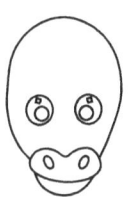

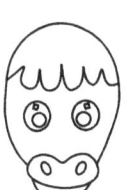

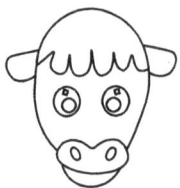

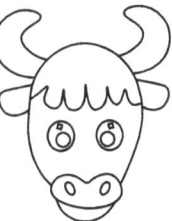

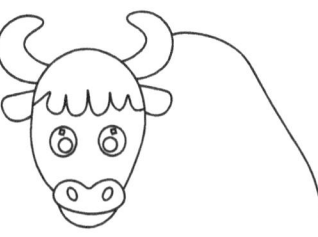

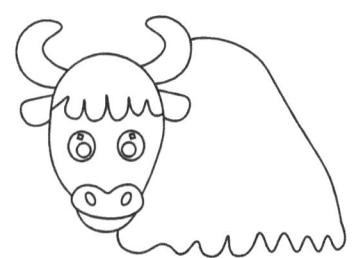

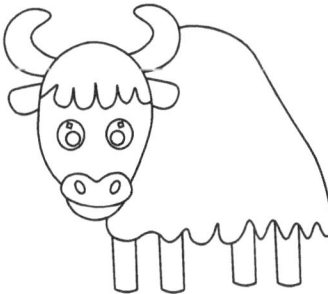

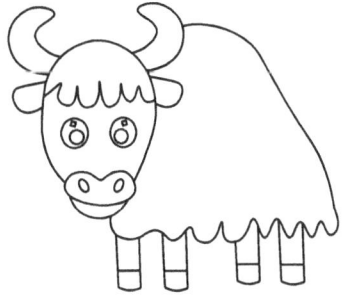

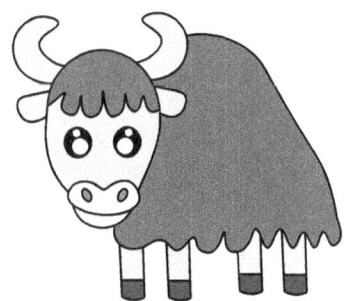

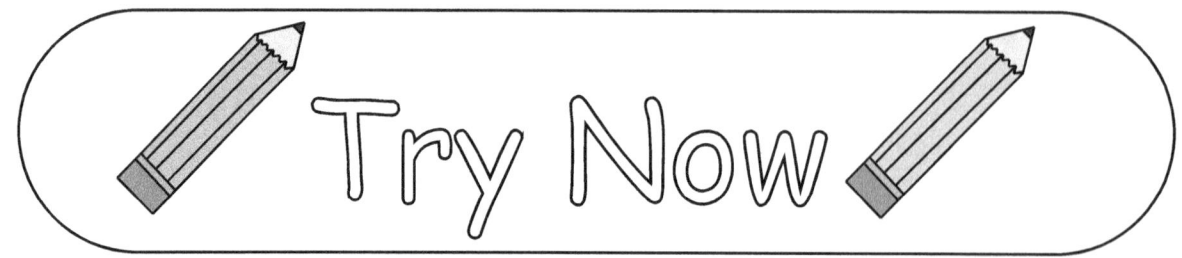

Ibex

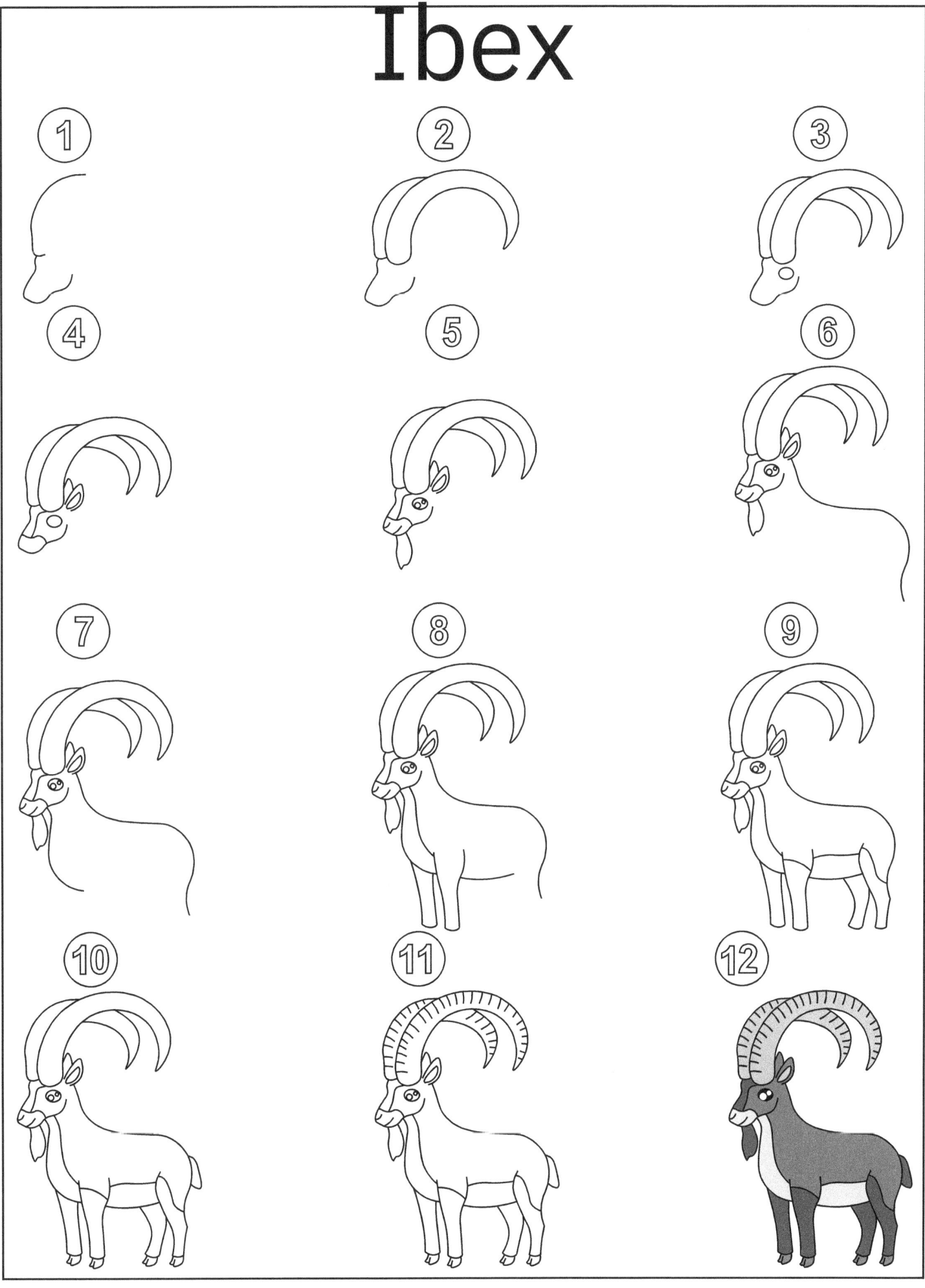

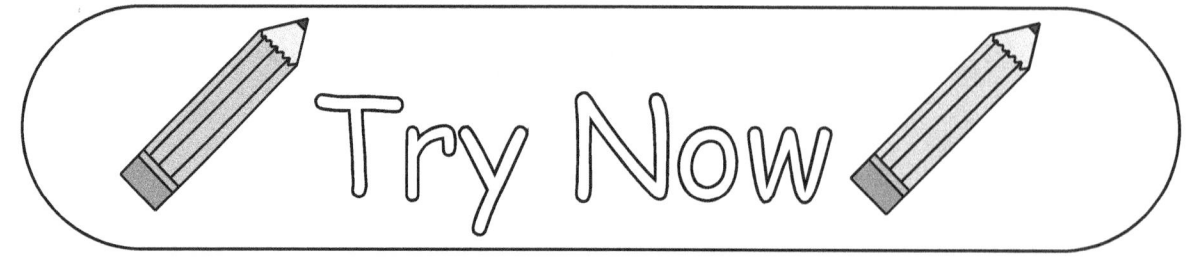

Iguana

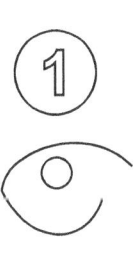

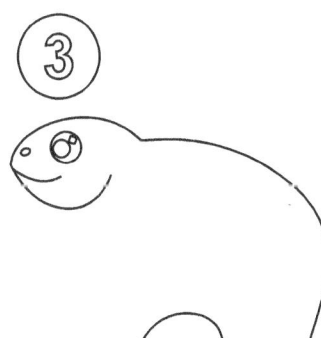

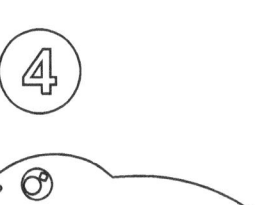

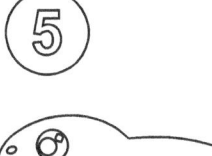

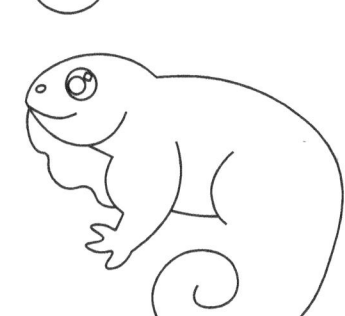

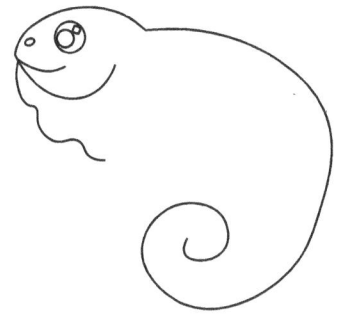

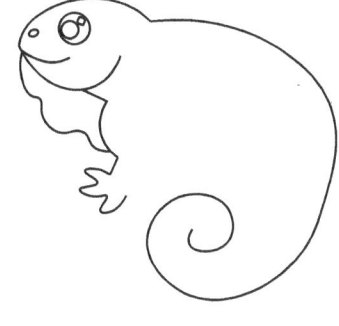

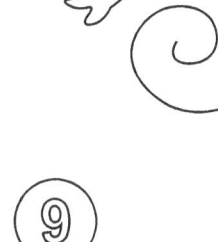

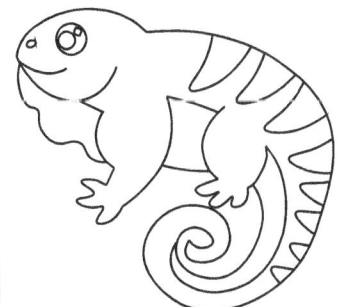

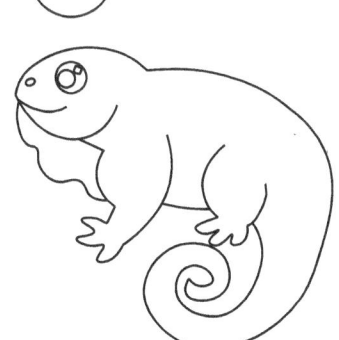
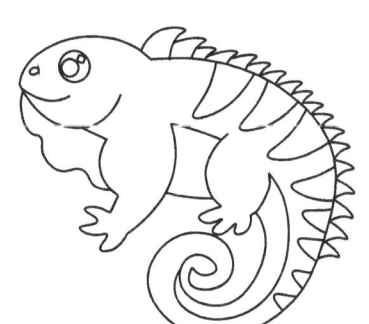

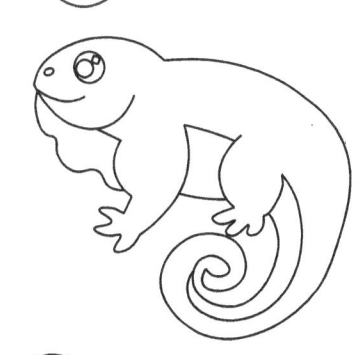

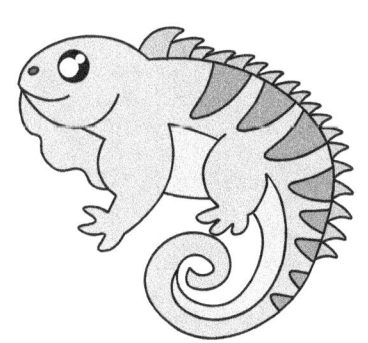

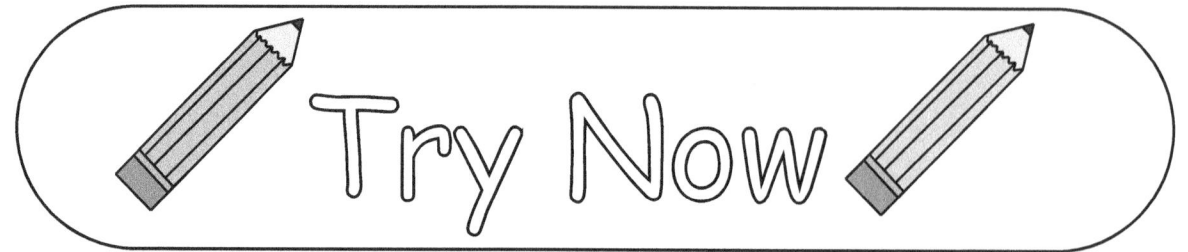

Otter

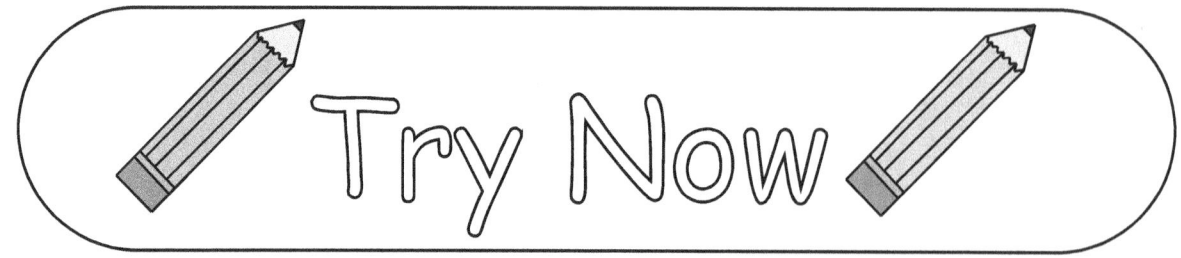

Beaver

 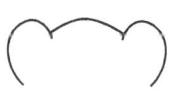

 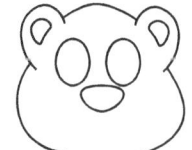

 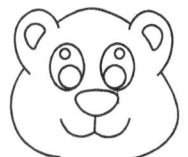

 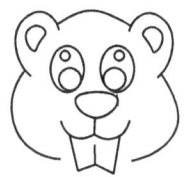

 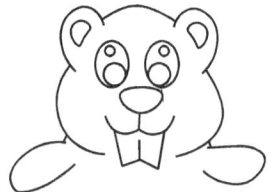

 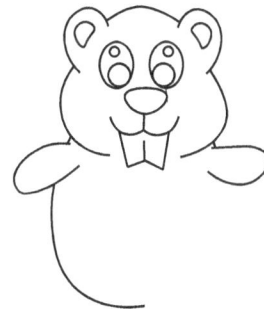

 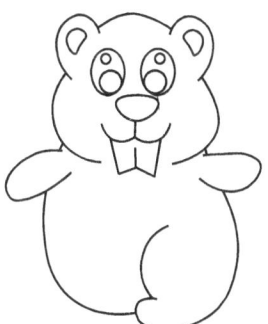

 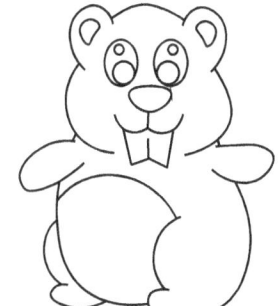

 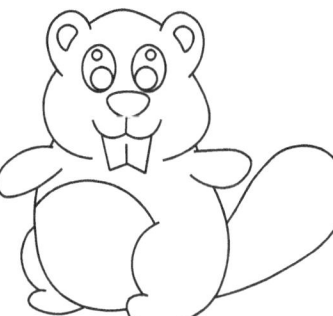

 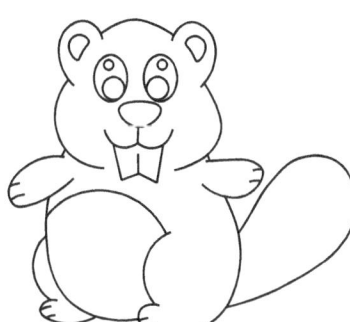

 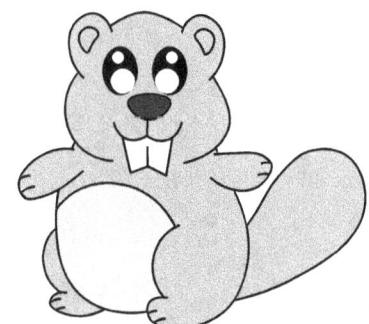

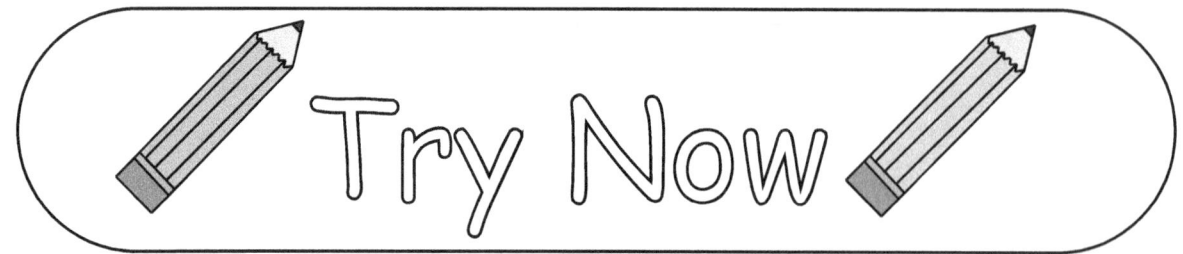

Bison

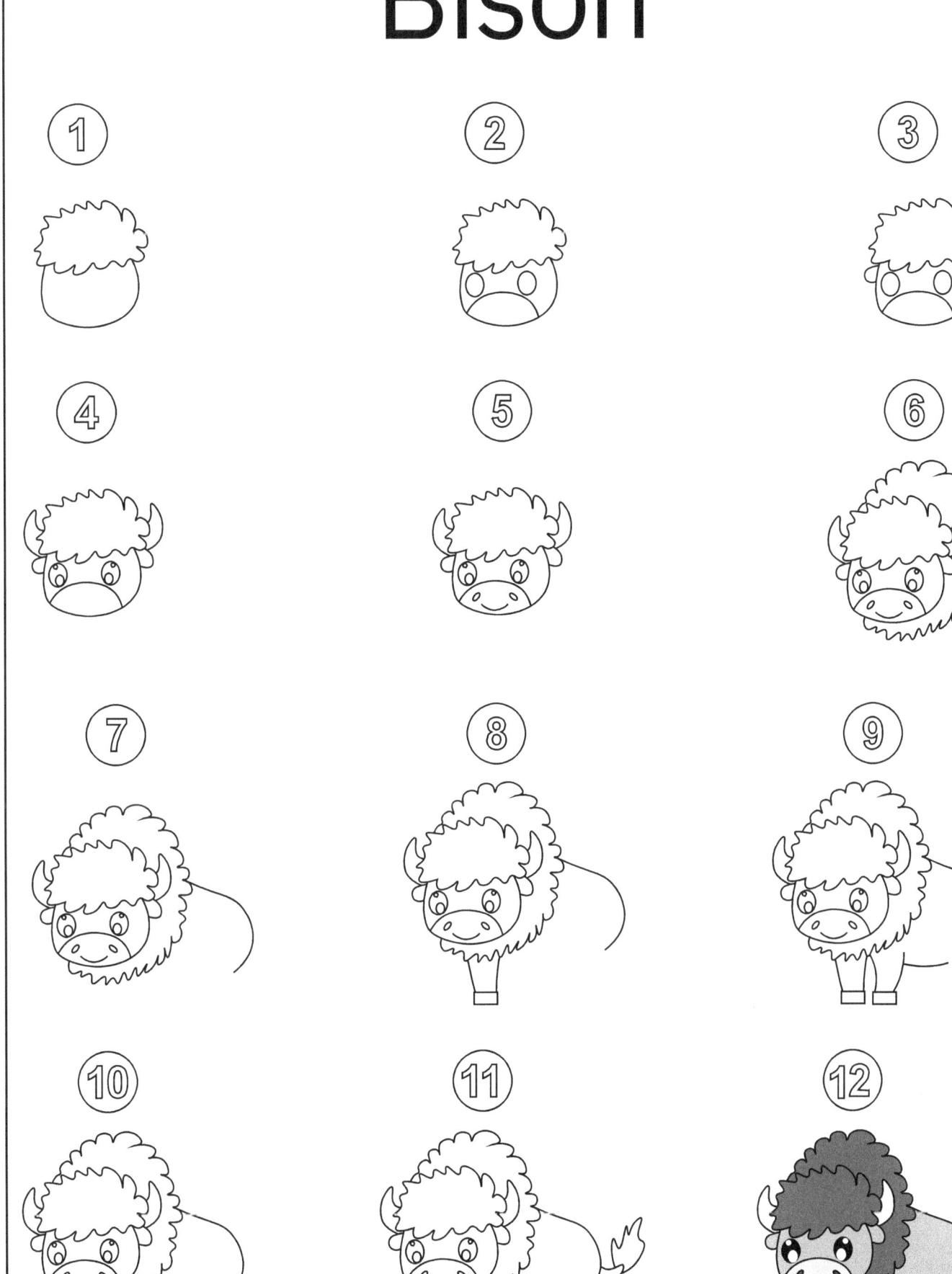

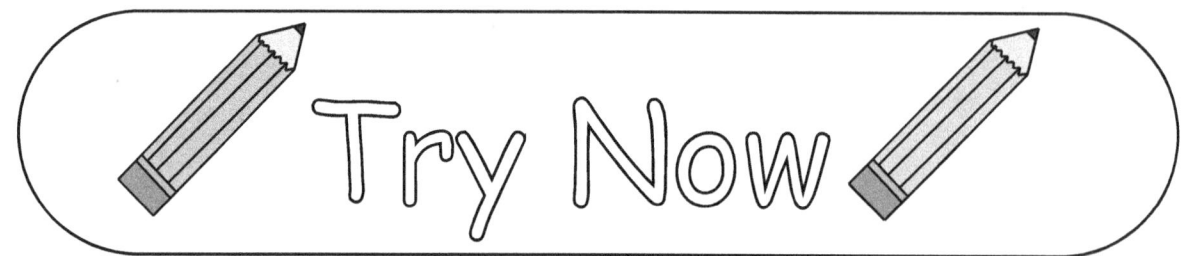

Try Now

Koala

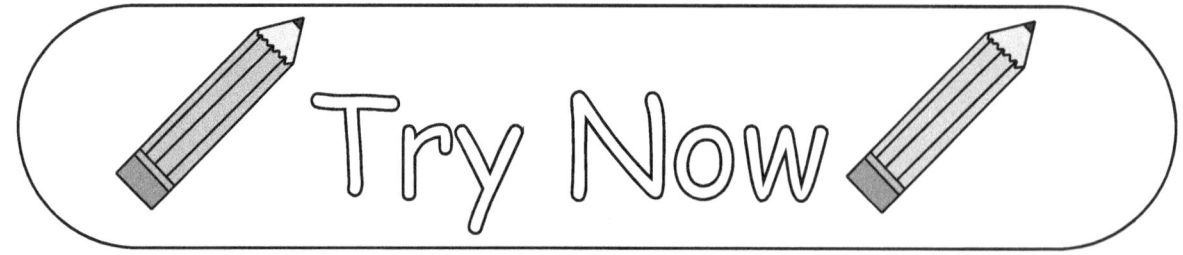

Sloth

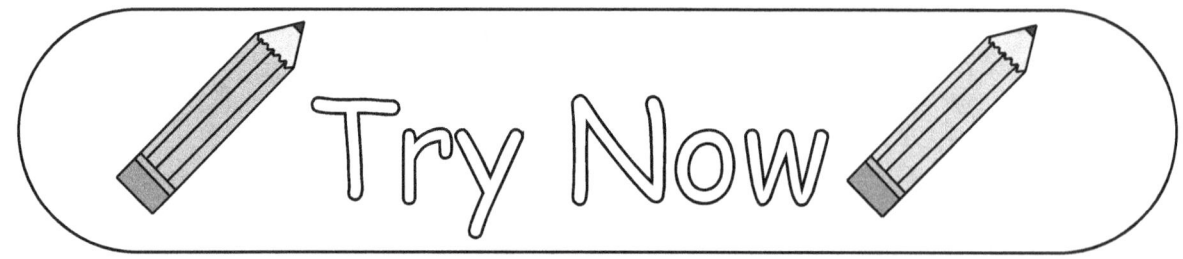

Try Now